IN Spite of

Published in the United States by Book Power Publishing, an imprint of Niyah Press, Detroit, Michigan.
www.bookpowerpublishing.com

Book Power Publishing books may be purchased for educational, business, or sales promotional use.

Contact the author at: Katrinareneawrites@yahoo.com

First Edition
PRINTED IN THE UNITED STATES OF AMERICA.

ISBN: 978-1-945873-38-6

Detroit, Michigan

Contents

Dedication

To my momma Carolyn, who I would have sworn
hung the moon and stars, and invented every word and
phrase. The one who taught me to read and fostered my
love of books. You are one of the most creative people
I know whether you are whipping up something in the
kitchen, making up games like "Grocery Store", or telling
us ghost stories that probably weren't appropriate for
children. You are one of my most favorite people.
I love you the biggest most.

To my siblings: Donald, Derrick, Moria, Jamal, Fallon,
and Mark. To my nieces and nephews Brittany, Jared,
Taylor, and Cheyenne; we've been through so much
together and survived it all. We've got stories and
more stories and I'm glad y'all are part of my story.
To my brothers Albert Jr. and Dillon,
we've got more memories to make.

KATRINA RENEA CARPENTER

IN Spite of

BOOK
POWER
PUBLISHING
Detroit, Michigan

MOTHER TO SON

BY <u>*LANGSTON HUGHES*</u>

Well, son, I'll tell you:
Life for me ain't been no crystal stair.
It's had tacks in it,
And splinters,
And boards torn up,
And places with no carpet on the floor—
Bare.
But all the time
I'se been a-climbin' on,
And reachin' landin's,
And turnin' corners,
And sometimes goin' in the dark
Where there ain't been no light.
So boy, don't you turn back.
Don't you set down on the steps
'Cause you finds it's kinder hard.
Don't you fall now—
For I'se still goin', honey,
I'se still climbin',
And life for me ain't been no crystal stair.

Prologue

There is a beautiful ignorance that comes with child-hood. You accept everything that comes your way and half the time you don't even know what the heck is going on. Within the bubble of my family, we had financial ups and downs, good times, and bad times, but at the end of it all we came out stronger and closer. We dealt with our struggles privately, but I think our private struggles are both entertaining and hopefully inspiring. We've come a long way and I want to share some of that journey with others who might benefit from seeing where I came from and the things I have been blessed to have achieved In Spite Of all the obstacles that were against me.

1. Broadway Avenue

"You almost killed me." "I can't eat anything when I'm pregnant, I was so small when I got to the hospital, the doctor couldn't believe I was really

1

9 months." Whenever we talk about the story of my birth, Momma loves to say how she was 35 and too old to be having another baby. I always say, "that's between you and Albert." She was extremely sick and had to be transported an hour away from Bowling Green, KY to Vanderbilt hospital in Nashville, TN. My parents weren't together when Momma got pregnant with me. Albert wasn't even at the hospital when I was born. Out of 8 babies, I was the only one born in Nashville, and the only one not born in February or March. I think that's why I'm the only sane one. When I was little, my older siblings Fallon and Mark loved to remind me I wasn't born in BG. One of the local hospitals used to run a commercial all the time "If You're a Medical Center baby please stand up." I would always happily jump up off the couch. They would quickly tell me, "You aren't a Medical Center baby; you weren't even born here, you were born in Nashville." I would get upset every time they said it. Momma wasn't alone in Nashville, my Aunt Mary Jo, the oldest of Momma's siblings, had her husband Uncle Mitchell drive her to the hospital, where she forced her way into the delivery room.

Somehow, her sisters convinced an exhausted, doped-up Momma to name me after my grandmother Mary Elizabeth. I went from Katrina Renea to Mary Katrina Renea. It's kind of cool how my family picks names. My grandmother Mary Elizabeth had 7 children Mary Jo-Jodie, Carolyn (my mom), Joe William-Joe, Douglas-Dougie, Australia-we pronounce it Ah stray yuh and sometimes the grownups would call her just Straya, Alfred Lane-Lanie and Regina-Gina, so that's 4 girls and 3 boys. They have a ton of other nicknames as well, Jodie Roll, Carolina Moon, Lil, Clean Up, and some I've forgotten. Momma had 8 children, 5 boys and 3 girls. Donald, Derrick, Michael (he died as a baby), Moria, Jamal, Fallon,

Mark, and then me, the baby, Katrina. We had our own nicknames as well, Moria is Tumble, Jamal is Poppa, Fallon is Tete and Fat Baby, Mark is Markie Dee and Twain, and Derrick is Gonzie. I think I probably have the most nicknames; Nadal Dee, Squirms, and Pudge.

Aunt Jo had been done having kids, and while Regina and Australia were both pregnant at the same time as Momma, they were days away from giving birth to boys Cornelius and Donald. None of them planned to have any more kids after that, I would be the last girl from my grandmother's daughters.

The crazy thing is my mom had a terrible relationship with her mother. Grandmomma had been both verbally and physically abusive to her as a child. All of Momma's sisters had fine curly hair that was easy to manage. Momma had thick, nappy hair and when her mother would comb it, she would yank her hair and neck around and threaten to cut her hair off. When my mom was 5 years old, her mother lost her job and didn't have any money. Her mother, Elsie Harpool, came to the house and told her that she would take all the kids to stay with her. This would allow her to get two jobs if she needed to and get back on her feet. Grandmomma said, "I can handle the rest of them, but Carolyn is the problem, you can take that little bitch." So, Momma got up and put her clean clothes in one paper sack and her dirty clothes in another paper sack. Then she sat and waited for her granny to come and get her.

Living with her grandma was night and day from life with her mother. Grandma Elsie had long hair with a skunk streak in the middle that she wore in a long braid down her back. On Saturday's, she would have it professionally curled so tight it looked like she had two inches of hair. It took two weeks for the curls to fall.

Elsie was a loving, religious woman, who taught Momma many things like being charitable. They would walk around the neighborhood and if they saw cutoff notices on someone's door, she would send Momma to take it. Then she would call her friends from church on a party line. A party line was a local telephone loop circuit that was shared by more than one subscriber. There was no privacy on a party line; if you were conversing with a friend, anyone on your party line could pick up their telephone and listen in. They would all chip in what they could, one person might have $1 and someone else $2.50 until they had enough to pay the bill. Back then the overdue bills weren't more than $15 or $20. Then great Grandma would go in the morning on her way to work and pay the person's bill so they wouldn't get cut off. She walked to work and worked from 6 a.m.-6 p.m. She only made $30 a day. She would also put groceries on people's porches. If someone died, all the church ladies would go clean and cook for the family even if they didn't want them to.

Her granny taught her how to cook, impressed upon her rules for life, like ladies always wear stockings to church and never pants. Momma had never had a birthday cake, but after she moved with her granny, she had her first one. Elsie had Momma taking a bath every night and washed her hair once a week. She made sure she was dressed for school, breakfast made, and lunch packed before she left for work at 5 a.m. Elsie, her granny, came to every school event, but Mary Elizabeth, her momma, didn't. Elsie had a treehouse in the backyard for Momma. She took good care of Momma until Momma had to take care of her.

Elise was diagnosed with cancer and when Momma was 10 years old, she died. The impact of her death was very deep for my mom. I remember her telling us that at the end her granny was crying out in pain, begging God to help her.

4

The only thing that helped were the morphine injections which Momma would give to her. As the pain grew worse she started to give her more and more morphine, above what was prescribed to help ease her pain. Dr. Beckett, the physician treating her, knew what my mother was doing and started giving her more morphine. The fact that God let her granny suffer such pain, despite her sincere belief in Him, affected Momma's beliefs about God. Because in her words, "How could a kind and loving God let her suffer." Her opinion was that if He existed, "He was a jealous and vengeful God," but she doesn't believe He exists.

After her grandmother died, Momma returned to living with her mom and siblings. It was not a happy transition. At Elsie's house, she could freely move about as she wanted and food was plentiful. Momma could eat breakfast, lunch, and dinner, and make a sandwich or grab a snack at her leisure. At her mother's house, they weren't even allowed to go in the fridge. Grandmomma worked at night, mostly in local clubs, so she would sleep really late. They couldn't eat anything until she woke up and cooked. Momma started getting headaches from not being able to eat, so one morning she went in the kitchen and started to cook. Grandmomma woke up and beat her and told her that was her food and her skillets, and she couldn't touch a thing. But after she ate the food, she told her, "Okay Momma taught you how to cook, so if you want to make breakfast from now on you can."

They weren't allowed to leave the house when Grandmomma left. But as soon as she went out the front door and turned the corner, they would sneak out the back door and meet up with Momma's best friend Nancy. Nancy taught Momma how to feed herself. Her and her brother Charles Melvin taught her how to steal everything from food to shoes and socks. They would take ham and

5

whole loaves of bread and squish it. There was no difference in the taste once it was flattened. They stole soda off the soda truck. They couldn't bring the stolen goods in the house, so in the wintertime they would bury it in the snow. Momma taught her brother Joe how to steal as well. Once they all went in the store wearing raggedy shoes and came out wearing brand new ones instead of those cheap skipjacks they had been wearing. They would steal things to appease Mary Jo as well, snack cakes, drinks, and magazines. Everything Mary Jo learned she taught Momma, she even taught her how to read using the True Confessions magazines they would steal for her.

Momma was a heavy child and was standing with a broom on Mary Jo's neck. Grandmomma had given Mary Jo money to buy food, but she would always buy bologna and Lottie soda. Momma hated bologna and Lottie soda tasted like cough syrup. Jo would buy crap for them so she could get good stuff for herself. The other kids ran and got Grandmomma. She came into the house and hit Momma in the head with the wash pan. She beat her so bad she was unconscious for days. Joe was sharp enough to pour water down her throat for several days until she regained consciousness. This wasn't the only time her mother physically attacked her. They only had a two-bedroom house, so Momma was sharing a bed with her mom. When Grandmomma came home and pulled back the blanket, she saw the sheets were covered in mud. She assumed that Momma had had a boy in her bed when really it was Mary Jo who caused the mud, so she took a broom and beat her in between the legs. She beat her until she was unconscious, then made her sleep outside. When my granny was in the hospital dying from cancer, she tried to apologize to Momma for the abuse. Momma would sneak her cigarettes and help her smoke in the bathroom. These are the kinds of stories I heard growing up which made it hard for me to like sharing her name.

The extent of my relationship with her was the occasional Sunday dinner at her house. She would cook these huge dinners, but then we had to wait for like an hour for the food to sit and "season" on the stove before we could eat. I also remember sitting on the floor in her living room while her and Momma talked with the TV on Soap Operas, Westerns, and the like. She was the only grandparent I ever knew since my dad's parents died when he was a kid and Momma never knew her father. I never liked the name Mary because I knew it was her name and I knew that Momma hated her. I dislike how many of my official documents bear that name. Mary Katrina Renea is written on everything from school paperwork to my college degrees to mortgage documents.

My first job was in a grocery store. Our old bookkeeper used to print my paychecks with my full name, and then required me to sign my full name every single time I cashed my check at the store. The name on my social security card and birth certificate don't even match because Momma didn't plan to name me Mary, so she signed one name on the birth certificate and a different one on the paperwork for Social Security, which complicates things when trying to get a driver's license or passport. It's so rare for me to use the name Mary so, whenever someone calls me on the phone and asks for Mary Carpenter or I call a company and they can't find my record because I am listed under Mary, I just involuntarily roll my eyes and my body stiffens a little. It's interesting that I have such a strong reaction because I didn't even have enough of a relationship with my grandmother to dislike or hate her. My feelings are solely based on what I have heard over and over from my Momma. I try to ignore the name Mary and focus on the rest of my name and the meanings behind each of them. The name Katrina is Greek/German and means"pure", Renea is Latin and means "born again or rebirth." When I can't ignore the name Mary, I tell myself there is beauty and honor attached to the name. Mary is in the Bible and Qur'an, it's Hebrew and means, "Of the Sea, Bitter, Beloved." She is the mother of Prophet Jesus and is highly revered. But in the end, I think about why I was given that name, and I'm reminded I don't have that same level of reverence for my own grandmother.

Ironically, I learned that my unplanned first name isn't one I share with just my mother's mom. My dad's mother was also named Mary Evelyn and his dad's name was Roland Hayes. Unfortunately, I never got the chance to meet either of them, since they both died when my dad was a kid. While my only knowledge of my grandma, Mary Elizabeth, is secondhand accounts of abuse and the sporadic Sunday dinner in a house with a room filled with white furniture we couldn't sit on, my knowledge and memories of my dad's mother, Mary Evelyn don't exist. My mom had to remind me of my paternal grandparents' names because I don't really think about them since I never knew them.

THE TEST

Katrina Carpenter, Age 3

The room was starkly white with bright lights. Momma held me as the nurse took my blood and I cried. My tears were partly because of the tension in the room and partly because I was afraid of needles. A man stood next to us, also getting his blood drawn. I remember crying. I clearly remember my crying. *I don't know how old I was, but I was young maybe 3 or 4. If someone asked me my first real memory of my dad, it would probably be the DNA test.*

Recently, my dad told me the reason he requested the DNA test. "I was facing a year in jail for nonpayment of child support. My lawyer told me that for the court to enforce the support order, they had to first prove paternity. Until they prove paternity, they can't prove that you owe the money and can't throw you in jail." It wasn't that he doubted he was my dad, in Momma's head she always thought he was trying to prove to her that he was the dad. While they may not have been able to throw him in jail that time, he did multiple stints in the Warren County jail over the years for failure to pay his court ordered support of a mere $100 a week.

Momma had a crush on my dad since she was a little girl. He lived next door with his grandparents. She would look at him across the fence and say, "I like you Albert, you're gonna be my boyfriend. Albert, you wanna be my boyfriend?" He would smile and laugh it off because he was a few years older than her. But he was always nice to her and would sometimes bring her treats like half of his popsicle.

By the time she was 12 and he was 15, they were sleeping together. It was the 60s. According to her, it was never a real boyfriend/girlfriend relationship. She always wanted to be with him, but he was always dating someone else, but when he wasn't she was his "in-between girl." The sexual attraction led to years of on again off again sexual encounters. The main reason their relationship didn't last was my dad's violent side. He wanted to control my mom and would stalk her movements and even abuse her physically.

NOT CO-PARENTING

My dad never lived with us after I was born and never attempted to coparent with my mother, although I don't think that term really existed in the 80s. He didn't come to see me or spend time with us at our house. I never went to his home to spend time with him or spend the night. I didn't experience every other weekend kiddie shuffle or summer breaks with Dad. I didn't do Thanksgiving with Momma and Christmas with Daddy. My dad was absent from my early childhood. Maybe I was lucky that he never made false promises to come and get me.

When I look at the relationship my stepdaughter has with her dad, it's like night and day. When I started talking to her dad, Victoria couldn't have been more than four. We would chat on the phone, and she would be giving commentary in the background. One day they were in the drive-thru getting food and she told me, "Sssh you have to be quiet now." She then proceeded to say, "Do you have sleepy-time clothes?" I had no idea what that meant until she explained, "You know it's what you sleep in." He would drive from Atlanta to Houston just to spend a week with her. He did the summer break parenting, bringing her from Houston to Atlanta for a month or two, but it wasn't enough. Before my husband and I decided to get married in 2014, he told me he wanted to move to Houston to be closer to his daughter and be more active in her life, so we did. He helped her learn to read, to ride a bike, and roller skate. He takes her skating, swimming, shopping, on vacation and pretty much anywhere she wants to go. Like all the other parents, he sold that damn school fundraiser candy to coworkers and neighbors because those kids aren't going to sell a thing. From parent teacher conferences to awards ceremonies, end of year programs, graduations, and talent shows, if she tells him about it, he is there.

Yet, she isn't always thrilled for her dad to be a dad. There's been times when she didn't want him to pick her up or would tell him she didn't want to come over and wanted to stay at home. When he gets involved in her schoolwork or fusses at her and holds her accountable for getting good grades and providing structure and expectations around her life and her education, she doesn't want it. One day during virtual learning, she got really upset with him for telling her she had to do her work at her desk, not lying in the bed in her pajamas. He wanted to create structure and normalcy for her even during the pandemic. She wanted to be lazy and attend class from bed, or even skip the first class of the day. He wasn't having it, so she got mad and ran out the front door into the cold morning air, setting off the security alarm. I went outside and brought her inside and asked her point blank what her problem was and what she was thinking. She basically said she couldn't be herself and do what she wanted to do which was sleep in longer and attend her class from the comfort of her bed. I had had enough, so I told her, "Listen, not every dad cares! Not every dad makes an effort to spend time with their kid, not every dad worries about how their kid is doing in school! My dad never picked me up or asked me about school, so when your dad is fussing at you or telling you what to do when it comes to schoolwork, you are lucky that he actually cares." After all that she calmed down and said, "Can you ask my dad to come back in and help me?"

I don't think she realizes just how blessed she is to have the dad that she does, even if he isn't perfect, He does a lot more than many dads I know. My dad came to one awards ceremony in middle school, and I think that was because Momma didn't have a car, so she asked him to drive her. He carried my backpack to the truck and asked me what I had in there. I never could figure out combination locks, so I carried all my books around every single day to every single class.

While I wasn't the child waiting for the phone to ring, and I didn't stare at the door or look out the window for a man who wasn't coming; I longed for him and wished for even a sliver of the kind of relationship Victoria has with her dad. I didn't know how to express it, but my actions reflected my desire to have my dad. Mind you, I've always known who my father was; though, there was actually a short time when I called someone else Dad.

MY OTHER DADDY

My mom has a habit of returning to former lovers. When I was 5 years old, she dated a man named Richard. Turns out he is my oldest brother Donald's dad. There is a 23-year age difference between Donald and I to give you a bit of clarity. He had already gone off to school by the time I was born. Richard was tall, thin, caramel colored, quiet, and kind. He lived with us for a while, off and on, and was a consistent presence in my life. I must have gotten it in my head that because he was a man, and he was always around, that he was my dad. I recall being in elementary school and having a field trip to the Capitol Arts Center where he worked. I excitedly told everyone in my class that my dad worked there. Once we got there, I cheerfully explained again that my dad worked there, not that I had any idea what his job was. On a second field trip to the Capitol Arts, we dipped our hands in different colored paint, then covered the wall in tiny kiddie handprints as part of a mural on the back of the building. I was quick to remind everyone that my dad worked there.

One day, he and my mom got into an argument, and she dropped him off at his house. I never knew why, and I don't remember exactly when, but one day he stopped being there. After that, no other man ever lived with us, and I lost the only semblance of a father figure I had.

2. Avon Avenue - Age 4/5

MOVING DAY

The landlord showed up in her pickup truck and started putting everything we owned in the back of it. Momma grabbed her big blue suitcase full of important papers like old report cards, award certificates, funeral programs, every single birthday, Mother's day, and holiday card she had ever received and garbage bags full of clothes. There was no neat and organized packing of boxes or loading up of a U-Haul truck. Everyone was moving around frantically, shoving whatever they could into the back of the station wagon. It had brown wood panels on the sides and back door with a huge window and plenty of cargo space. It was bright and sunny outside and, being four years old and too little to help, I stood watching all the action.

We got in the car and Momma drove away from our house on Avon Ave. The street name always stuck with me because my Momma loves Avon perfume and skincare products. She's fond of covering herself in a cloud of the warm floral scent of Odyssey Cologne, rubbing her cocoa brown skin with the fresh fragrance of *Skin So Soft* body oil and topping it all off with their liquid deodorant in the little square glass bottles with the Tiffany Blue plastic top and matching label. Her routine leaves the combination of wonderful scents hanging in the air for hours after she has left the room. My first Avon scent was the perfect choice for a little girl, *Sweet Honesty*. It came in a clear glass bottle with pink script letters and a light pink top, so this connection to my mom and perfume solidified my memory of living on a street named Avon.

We drove around town for hours and hours, not going anywhere in particular. We even drove past my Aunt Australia's apartment building out on Barren River Road. The area was surrounded by woods and the single dark grayish brown building set back off the road seemed to be towering on stilts it was so high. You had to climb wooden stairs to get to her apartment. There wasn't the typical paved parking lot or a driveway, instead there was gravel everywhere from the edge of the road all the way up to where the apartment building sat. For some reason, we didn't stop at my auntie's house, instead Momma kept driving. We didn't go to my Uncle Dougie's house either. I used to go there a lot so his wife Aunt Diddy Bop could babysit me while Momma worked. Uncle Dougie always picked on me, calling me a little boy and threatening to give me Indian feet. I had no clue what that meant, but it sounded bad. We didn't go to Uncle Joe's house either. He was the uncle that would come over to the house happily tipsy after working hard painting houses, sometimes still in his work clothes and say, "Katrina," in his deep voice, then pick me up and touch my body to the ceiling. It was easy for him since he is a good 6 feet and some change tall. He loved to bring us sweets and then leave just as quickly as he had come. We didn't go to Aunt Jo's house either and we didn't go to Grandmomma's, which wasn't surprising because Momma didn't have that kind of relationship with her. The mood of the car ride was tense and extremely quiet. We drove so long it got dark and I fell asleep.

When I woke up the next morning, we were at the trailer that my older brother Derrick shared with his friend Dickie. It was a small trailer, not made for 2 adult men, a grown woman, five children, and two grandbabies. We couldn't comfortably stay there for long, plus it wouldn't be fair to impose our huge family on Dickie. After a few days, Momma got her paycheck, and we were off to our next temporary home.

Music has always been a big part of my life. Growing up, we listened to everything Momma loved from Boy George, Patsy Cline, Aretha Franklin, and Anita Baker. We listened to artists from the 90s like En Vogue, SWV, and Blackstreet. But when I think about our life and the move from Avon and the many moves that followed, one song comes to my mind; *Temporary Home*, by Carrie

Underwood. It relates the stories of various people going through transitions in life. There are a couple of lines that specifically talk about a mom needing help and having nowhere to go. Being abruptly evicted from our home, not knowing where or who to turn to, and then having to move again and again could have been an additional verse in Carrie's song. While the song speaks to the difficult life circumstances the various individuals were experiencing, each person responded to their situation with optimism *in spite of* not knowing exactly what the future held. It leaves you feeling optimistic that even if you aren't where you want to be, the situation is temporary.

THE TOPPER MOTEL, BOWLING GREEN, KY

The sign out front had a black top hat like a magician's. Underneath were the words Topper in white letters and Motel in red. It was a roadside motel out on the 31 W Bypass, the kind where when you opened the door to your room you were in the parking lot. It was the first time I'd been in a motel. For me it was a fun and exciting experience, like being on vacation; not that we had ever been on vacation. There was no kitchen, so instead of Momma cooking dinner and everyone eating at the table, we got to eat fast food and junk food while sitting in bed watching cable. We all slept in the same room in two full size beds. Walking to the ice machine outside gave us a little break from the room.

We were on this extended vacation for several months. In my youthful innocence, it didn't register that this hotel adventure wasn't one of choice. At 5 years old, I didn't have the concept of homelessness. I was just caught up in the newness of the situation and content being with my family. After being unexpectedly forced out of our home with little more than the clothes on our backs and a few important papers, we had nowhere else to go. We were stuck in the hotel because a single mother, a single black mother with lots of kids living paycheck to paycheck couldn't just pick up and start over. Not many landlords were eager to rent to someone with a large family. They were even less eager to rent to someone freshly evicted from their last home. Never mind if that eviction wasn't fair and might today be considered illegal. It took time to find a landlord that would work with our situation and to save up enough money to move to a real home.

DENNIS WAY

Bang. Bang. Bang. Bang. Bang. "Come in," Momma said, just as a random white man opened the front door and walked inside. He started walking through the house like he owned it. He went into the kitchen and began opening the cabinets, then headed for the first bedroom. Momma rushed to the bedroom ahead of him, grabbed the gun from under her pillow, and pointed it at him. "Who the hell do you think you are walking through my damn house?" "I just bought this house and I have the right to inspect it and you have one week to get out." "Well until I do, this is my house and you need to get out." It was summertime and we had only been living in the house for about one school year. The landlord had never mentioned he was selling the house, let alone had already sold the house to someone else. The new owner became belligerent, arguing with

Momma and telling her he was former military special forces. The landlord showed up and the police came and told him he was in the wrong and had to go through the courts. Once they went to court, we were given 30 days to move instead of the one week the new owner had wanted. We were being kicked out with basically no notice and for no reason. Once again, we had to hastily move.

3. Fair Street- Age 5/6

WARNING: THE LORD AND LIQUOR DO NOT MIX!!

"Our Father, who art in heaven, hallowed be thy Name. Thy Kingdom come. Thy will be done on earth, as it is in heaven. Give us this day our daily bread. And forgive us our trespasses, as we forgive those who trespass against us. And lead us not into temptation but deliver us from evil. For thine is the kingdom, the power, and the glory, forever and ever. Amen."

It was a Saturday afternoon and Momma and my Aunt Australia had been hanging out at the neighborhood spot. Somehow, they got on the topic of *The Lord's Prayer* because you know everyone is thinking about God at the bar. Momma said it went one way, and my aunt said it went another. To settle the debate, they came back to our house. For some inexplicable reason, my mother, a self-proclaimed atheist, had several decorative china plates with the Lord's prayer and other popular religious quotes and scriptures written on them hanging on the wall above the kitchen door. They came in arguing loudly; my aunt was drunk. Momma immediately sent all of us kids to one of the front bedrooms and told us not to come back out. We were of course listening intently inside the room. The writing on the plate proved Momma right but instead of ending the debate things got physical.

My auntie was mad that Momma always thought she was right about everything. Momma tends to be the one everyone turns to for help or advice amongst her siblings. Momma, of course, wasn't going to let it go when she knew she was right. Hell, she probably wouldn't have let it go if she had been wrong. Aunt Australia never weighed more than 90 pounds soaking wet, she was a little Chihuahua with the heart of a crazy Pitbull, never afraid to fight. Momma, on the other hand, was always 180 pounds or better and could mop the floor with my aunt. The fight got out of hand and Momma ended up pushing auntie through the window, breaking glass outside and into the room.

Once she decided my aunt had had enough, Momma told my brother Derrick to drive her home. With her weekend cleanup music on blast, she went to work sweeping up the mess with her back to the front door. We were all still confined to the bedroom and happened to be looking out the window, when out of nowhere we saw Australia marching up the front walkway with a tire iron or metal pipe in her hands, high above her head. We were told not to leave the room and we did not disobey. The only thing we could do was yell, "Momma, Momma, Australia is coming, she's got something," as loud as possible, hoping to be heard over the music and the sound of broken glass. We didn't even think to open the door and warn her.

Australia barged inside yelling, "You shouldn't have done this to me, you shouldn't have done this to me." I don't know if Momma heard us, heard my aunt come in the door, or if her intuition made her turn around, but she did just in the nick of time. She was able to wrestle the piece of metal from my aunt and prevent being cold cocked in the head. Moments later, my brother came back and explained that when he stopped the car, Australia had jumped out and ran back toward the house before he could stop her. I guess since she had lost round one, she had decided she needed a weapon.

Momma and Australia were thick as thieves. They would go grocery shopping together and me and DonDon would be right beside them pushing our own little carts. They cooked dinner for each other's family and loved to get dressed up. Clean Up was my aunt's nickname because she cleaned up nice when she went out. Hell, they were even pregnant at the same time. My mom gave birth to me on September 10, and my aunt gave birth to my cousin Donald on September 20th. Their close relationship meant me and DonDon were close, spending as much time together as our moms did and of course having play dates where we created our own language and had little adventures while climbing over rolls of carpet from the neighborhood carpet store that were kept in an 18-wheeler beside auntie's house. Despite their unbelievable closeness, at least once a year they always had a big blow-up fight. Who would have thought this time it would be over *The Lord's Prayer*? Side note: It turns out there are at least two versions of *The Lord's Prayer*, so maybe my aunt just knew a different version.

Fair Street was a house full of good memories too. I have pictures of me, my sister Fallon, my brother Mark, and my niece Brittany, all in our winter coats looking like extras from the movie *A Christmas Story*, standing in front of a floor model TV. This was the house where I learned to share not just my toys with my niece, who is only 3 years younger than me, it wasn't just my little red wagon or red tricycle with black and white tires, it was ours, but I also learned to share my momma. I have a cute picture of my cousin Shavon, my brother Mark, me, and my momma holding my nephew, Jared. Momma swears it's not her in the picture, but she is holding my hand and I was a total Momma's girl. I don't think I would have let some random lady hold my hand. We somehow managed to take family photos over the years at home or even better in professional studios, like JCPenney, Sears, or Olan Mills. For some reason, Momma was usually not in the picture.

Bottom left Jared Carpenter, Brittany Carpenter,
Katrina Carpenter...Middle Moria Carpenter, Mark,
Carpenter, Jamal Carpenter and Fallon Carpenter

Bottom left Katrina Carpenter and Brittany Carpenter
Top Mark Carpenter and Fallon Carpenter

Back Left to Right-Shavon Bowman,
Brittany Carpenter, Carolyn Carpenter
Bottom Left to Right-Mark Carpenter
and Katrina Carpenter

CAMP RAINBOW

There was also a neighborhood church that kept us busy in the summer with what they called Camp Rainbow. My sister thinks they only came up with the camp to get us kids involved in the church. We would walk there from our house and do different activities all centered around learning about God and the Bible. They always provided us with little snacks and lemonade. I don't remember ever attending a Sunday service at the church, just the camp. One afternoon, I was sitting on a stump in front of the church, when suddenly I felt like my butt was burning. There was a colony of fire ants in the stump, and they were attacking me. We had to rush home so I could get cleaned up.

Fair Street was the house where I practiced my artistic side, clicking my dress shoes as fast as I could, mimicking the great Gregory Hines. I had these beautiful red dress shoes that I would put on, then tap, tap, tap all over the house. I loved the sound my shoes made on the kitchen floor, until the day I fell flat on my back right in front of the fridge on the freshly waxed floor. It was the house where I sassed my sister Moria over my love for chocolate covered Whoppers candy. We were standing outside on the sidewalk, and I curtly told her I would jack slap her if she ate my candy. I don't even know where I heard the phrase "jack slap." I was spoiled rotten, Momma let me do and have whatever I wanted, and my siblings hated it. I wasn't a bad kid, I was the baby, her favorite, and everyone knew it. Whenever she would leave the house, Momma would tell them, "I'm leaving and y'all better not fuck with her while I'm gone." Then I would run off and hide under her bed.

We stayed there for quite a while until Momma's boss Stan at Dozier's restaurant offered her a high paying job as the head cook at another restaurant; JB Danes in South Pittsburg, Tennessee. She hyped the move up as this great opportunity for all of us. She took us to a salon and had the stylist give us all Jheri Curls, then we were on the road to a new state.

4. South Pittsburg, TN - Age 6

"Music is the soundtrack of your life." —*Dick Clark*

I f my life had a soundtrack, then the song *My Ding a Ling* by Chuck Berry would represent the cringey time we spent in Tennessee. South Pittsburg was the first and only place I ever heard that song. It was the creepiest song we had ever heard, and every time it came on the radio, we freaked out. It is one of the main things I associate with living in South Pittsburg. Tennessee was a big change from what we were used to in Bowling Green. Those Jheri Curls ended up being an epic failure, Jamal had to shave all my hair off, and I ran around looking like a little boy with a fade. Everything and everyone seemed to operate slower. I could read before I started kindergarten and was in the 1st grade when we moved. The school we attended asked us to bring in school supplies such as tissue and paper towels. We also had to cover our books. These things are all common today but back then it wasn't the norm in Bowling Green. The things they were teaching us in 1st grade were things I had been taught the year before in kindergarten, and I was very vocal about it. I didn't feel like I was learning anything new at all; I was bored.

The town itself was small and boring. The only place we could go was the neighborhood park complete with a basketball court. Our house was beautiful and sat up on a mountain side. My sister Moria was tasked with doing the laundry and hanging it out on the clothesline in the backyard to dry. At some point she stopped doing the laundry, and when my mom fussed at her for not getting it done, she claimed she had seen the eyes of an animal outside. Momma, assuming she was lying or being lazy, went outside that evening to do it herself. Suddenly, she came running in the house. A mountain lion had climbed down the mountain and was standing in the backyard. One of the ladies that lived next door had warned her not to hang out laundry at night because of the mountain lions, but she didn't take her seriously. After that, we could only do laundry in the daytime.

Other eyes were focused on our house. One day Fallon and I were getting dressed in the bedroom and noticed someone peeping in the window watching us. We screamed and the person ran off. Turns out Josh, the neighbor's kid who was friends with Mark, was a peeping Tom and had been peeping in our windows. Momma swiftly put the fear of hot lead in his butt, and we didn't have any more visits after that.

My brother Mark was a big fan of action movies and decided to create his own action figure out of aluminum foil. He then placed the foil man in the microwave, turned it on, and promptly caused the lights to go out; not just in our house but in the whole neighborhood. I think that was the only time our lights were out and not for failure to pay the bill.

Tennessee's promise of better opportunities, more money, and better living circumstances didn't pan out. Our house was nice, but it was in government housing. Stan and Darla, the owners of the restaurant, were supposed to move us into a real house and give Momma a better salary, but they didn't keep their promises. She was working 12-hour days, 7 days a week. Jamal was 15 and lied about his age so he could work with her and between the two of them they were running the restaurant. The staff Momma had to work with were incompetent. Once she told one of the assistant cooks to boil her a dozen eggs. The girl boiled a pot of water then proceeded to crack 12 eggs and dump them into the water.

Jamal got in trouble for messing around with some white girls in the next county over, this wouldn't have been a big deal in Bowling Green, but it wasn't acceptable in the area we were living in. Momma had to go to court with him because they were trying to prosecute him. Her boss Stan explained that the situation was dangerous and that they might try to hurt him, cut off his genitals, or even kill him if he kept messing with white girls. He told her they might spare him because they knew she was the good cook from Kentucky, but it was getting dangerous. She started making him stay in the house to protect him, but he thought she was punishing him for getting in trouble. She ended up winning $4,000 from the lottery around the time all this trouble started. Then when she and Jamal went to cash their checks at the store they had always gone to, the cashier cashed her check for $1000, but refused to cash Jamal's $500 check. She realized then, they were starting to watch him and must know about the issue with the white girls. Her boss Stan had to come to the store to get them to cash his check. After that, she told Jamal we were moving back to Kentucky. That weekend she rented a U-Haul and packed up the boxes while Jamal dismantled the furniture and loaded up the truck by himself. We didn't have anybody there to help us, so we had to leave a lot of big furniture, including a white sofa and brand-new Maytag washer and dryer.

We had to drive across the mountain to get from Tennessee to Kentucky, and Momma wanted to make the drive before it got dark because she was scared to drive in that area by herself, and she wasn't comfortable driving on the highway. Moria was 18 and pregnant with her third baby when our mom decided it was time to leave. Momma drove to where she was staying with her boyfriend and told her we were going back to Bowling Green. She chose to stay in South Pittsburg. Jamal was 16 by the time we left, so she had him drive the U-Haul and she drove her car. He led the way across the mountain and Momma followed behind him in her car. They stayed in the middle lane the whole time, she wanted to be in the right lane, not me. Jamal led us to Bowling Green, stopped to get food at the Dairy Queen, then went straight to Ms. Peggy's and parked the U-Haul behind her house. We went inside and fell asleep wherever we could.

5. Adams Street
X2-Age 7 and 8

The move back to Kentucky was not perfectly planned. When we first got back, we didn't have our own home, so we ended up staying with a family friend, Peggy D.

Momma had been friends with her and her family for years, and she invited us to stay with them until we could get our own place. Ms. Peggy was one of Momma's closest friends and since I was always with my Momma, I got to spend a lot of time with her. She taught me how to make biscuits from scratch using flour and water. She showed me how to lay a small layer of flour on the countertop then mold the dough into a mound. We used a glass to push into the dough to create the perfect round shape. She was also the first person to take me on an overnight trip with her boyfriend Tink. Peggy was the manager of the Hardee's restaurant and she got Momma a job with her. Momma was paying Peggy 100 a week for rent. She didn't want Peggy to know she had any extra money, so she was stealing food and supplies for the entire house and cooking every night after work. Peggy cooked on Sunday's. Momma washed the entire household's clothes every single day.

Peggy had three kids of her own, so there wasn't a lot of room for a whole extra family. Remember we were not a small family; my mom, two daughters, two sons, and two grandbabies. We slept on pallets on the floor in the living room and kitchen. I was unfazed by the unconventional living arrangements which only lasted a few months. Momma hit $1000 at Bingo and then we moved up the road from Peggy to a house on Adams Street.

We lived in two different houses on the same street. The first house was light blue and had a big front porch, the other house was right next door. It was red brick with white columns on the front porch. I think one of the houses was haunted. There was a closet that was shared by two rooms, just like how hotels have the door in between two rooms. I remember opening the door from one room, walking through, and getting the creepiest feeling when I walked through the closet to the other room. I think it

36

was the brown one because some other odd stuff happened there, like the missing money.

BINGO BLESSINGS

It had to be after 10 p.m. when Momma came into the house yelling excitedly. We all rushed to the living room to see what was going on. "I won, I won," she yelled and then threw her hands up in the air sending money flying around and then raining down on us. She had been at BINGO, one of her favorite pastimes, and had hit big; a $1,000 game. She was lucky like that, always winning at BINGO and hitting big, playing the Kentucky lottery numerous times. There's a picture of her holding one of those large lottery winner checks still wearing her work uniform and apron. We happily began helping her pick up the money from around the room. She told us how much she had won and started counting out the bills. As she counted, something was wrong, she was coming up short. The amount she had at home was a few hundred dollars less than the amount she had left the BINGO parlor with. As she counted and recounted, the numbers still weren't adding up. We looked all over the living room and couldn't find the rest of the money. We even brought in a chair from the kitchen so she could check the globe on the ceiling light, in case a little of the rain money had landed there. No more money could be found anywhere. Momma didn't have a car and she thought maybe the money had fallen out in the car of the friend that drove her home. Eventually, we all went to bed happy but confused. The next morning, we resumed our search for the missing money, including dragging a kitchen chair under the light fixture and checking for trapped money. This time there were several bills inside the globe bringing the total winnings back to the post BINGO/ pre money rain total. Nobody knows how the money got there when it wasn't there the night before. Momma and Tete don't even remember us using the chair to check the first night. Momma swears she smelled the money burning the next morning.

Katrina Carpenter

My niece Brittany and I used to go outside in our socks and "days of the week" undies, run across the porch, and back before coming inside. This was all in the 90s when we still thought every man in a station wagon or beige van was a pedophile waiting to snatch us, yet this silly routine amused us. I was in elementary school and loved having my picture taken on picture day, especially with the different backgrounds they would use, like the city skyline that didn't look anything like our downtown or the little props. I had a habit of taking every single picture with a huge smile showing my snaggle teeth and my shoulders scrunched up to my head and neck. When I came home, I had my siblings help me stage our own backdrops with these ugly brown curtains and a small white vase with a red rose in it and teddy bears, so that we could take pictures at home like they did for school photos. I loved taking pictures, so Momma would buy me disposable Kodak cameras. They went months and months before I could get them developed and when we would finally drop them off at the pharmacy to get them developed, I couldn't wait to pick up the finished product.

Top: Taylor Carpenter and Jared Carpenter
Bottom Katrina Carpenter

Brittany Carpenter

Katrina Carpenter

40

Living on Adams was very convenient since we didn't always have a car, we could easily walk to the neighborhood grocery store, Diemer's D & F SuperMarket. D&F was one of those stores that gave out those S & H green stamps at checkout. I remember licking those yucky stamps then trying to place them perfectly on each individual square of the collection sheet. Eventually filling up the sheets. I had no idea what the stamps were for, but I enjoyed the process of filling up the sheet. I would always walk to the store with my sister Fallon, sometimes we took my niece Brittany, but we usually left her little brother Jared at home. One day, we walked to the store and left him at the house. He was a toddler at the time and somehow got out of the house and tried to follow us to the store. Thankfully our neighbor, Vito Tisdale, yes, the one from Nappy Roots, happened to come outside and saw him walking by himself and took him back to the house. This was several years before the group got started, when he was just Vito, our neighbor and my brother Jamal's friend.

CREATIVITY IN THE KITCHEN

The Internet has made struggle meals famous; honestly half the stuff they consider struggle meals are high class compared to the kind of struggles we faced. This went beyond having peanut butter but no jelly. Bread but no meat. Kool-Aid but no sugar. We had days where we sat with our guts growling trying to think of something to eat and nights where we went to bed hungry. Our go to struggle snack was probably a tie between buttered bread with a sprinkle of sugar or bread and syrup for a full-blown meal. We were shoveling down bowls of brown beans with sugar and cornbread. I don't know why in the hell we put sugar in beans, but it tastes delicious. There is probably one struggle meal you've never heard of, the delicacy known as hotdog salad. I'm guessing no, since it was the desperate invention of two kids. My big brother Jamal was supposed to be babysitting my cousin DonDon and I while our moms were at work. We were starving and needed him to fix us breakfast. Jamal was a heavy sleeper; we tried to wake him up multiple times to fix us pancakes and he said he would, but he never got up. We decided we had to fend for ourselves, so we rummaged through the fridge and found the only thing we could fix was hotdogs. We chopped up hotdogs and pickles, then drizzled on mustard as a nice dressing and thus we had hotdog salad. I'm pretty sure that was the first and last time we ever ate it.

Momma was much more creative when it came to new recipes. She would turn leftovers into exotic dishes like Golash Danielle and Turkey Hash which is the next best thing to Thanksgiving dinner. We weren't living on Adams at the time, but this is another example of her culinary creativity. One night, Fallon had a friend sleeping over and we were all hanging out in her room. We smelled something delicious coming from the kitchen and Momma was making these perfectly seasoned messy burgers. She had mixed a can of Manwich, hamburger, chili seasoning, and some other spices and made what she called "Mexican Burgers." These were some of the best sandwiches we had ever eaten, and she made them maybe one more time. Then after a while, we asked her to make those Mexican Burgers again and she said, "I was high when I came up with that recipe and I don't remember what I put in them." She never could remember, and she never recreated those tasty sandwiches again.

Momma had some kitchen failures as well. We usually would clear our plates of whatever deliciousness she had prepared, but that did not apply to the day she made hominy. Hominy looks like corn, and you can buy it in a can just like regular corn, but it's processed differently and it tastes terrible. We tried to eat this corn phony, mixing it with other items on our plate, but none of us could get it down. So, Momma told us we couldn't get up from the table until we did. It must have been more than an hour later and none of us had finished the pile of yellow mush. Eventually, she came back into the kitchen and told us, "Y'all don't have to eat it, I accidentally bought hominy. I thought it was corn." The story is funny to me because we all held firm and none of us got in trouble and none of us ate it.

Momma made another meal I knew I wouldn't like, cabbage and potatoes. I told her multiple times I don't like cabbage, but she put it on my plate and then just like with the hominy standoff, told me I couldn't get up from the table until I ate it. Well, I got tired of sitting there, so I tried to eat a spoonful of the cabbage and even managed to swallow it. But I guess my mind and my tastebuds over-ruled me and I proceeded to puke up the entire meal across the dining room table. Momma yelled, "God damnit," and then dismissed me from the table.

WHITE PICKUP TRUCK

We walked all over town growing up, from the grocery store to doctors' appointments, to the unemployment office where we sat while Momma applied for jobs. We also walked to visit family or to the park. Everywhere we wanted or needed to go, we would walk to get there. I would trail along beside my siblings. We spent a lot of time at *High Street Community Center* which ironically was located on Center Street. We would walk the short mile (which didn't seem so short to my little legs) from our house on Adams Street to the community center and back. We would climb across the shiny train tracks with dark brown wood slats bolted in the middle and gravel stones in between, we would then walk past the big two-story red brick RC Cola offices and bottling plant. Sometimes during these walks, my oldest sister Moria would spot my dad's white pickup truck and yell, "Albert, Albert"until he stopped. Once we reached his truck, she would always say, "Give us some money Albert," or ask him to give us a ride. He would hand out dollar bills and let us climb in the back of his pickup truck. It was fun riding in the back with the wind blowing on our faces. I never thought to try and talk to him, and he didn't say anything to me. We just climbed in the back, and he took us wherever Moria told him to. These random interactions were the extent of my early relationship with my dad, *my second real memory.*

There are a few things my mom has always loved about my dad aside from their sexual chemistry which is her favorite. She always talked about how intelligent he was and how easily he could figure things out. He has always been good with his hands, able to build anything, from small home repairs to complete remodels. For years he owned his own small business, *Hayes Home Repair.* His company logo was so dope. It was all red and the letters made the shape of a house. The A was the roof, and the H was the base of the house. Momma would also tell us how creative and talented he was, like the way he decorated their only apartment together. He took a plain run of the mill apartment and upgraded it completely with blue and orange walls and even sewed the window curtains himself.

The beauty of the apartment was short lived. They had been living together for about a year and Momma was pregnant, but she wasn't sure if it was his baby or another man she was also messing with at the time. According to her, she did what she had to do to provide for her family.

44

Albert was mad about the uncertainty and not knowing if it was his baby or somebody else. Every time she left for work at night, he would break in and tear up the house. One night she hid in the house, without him knowing she was there. He climbed in the window, and she shot at him right across his shoulder. She could have killed him. She was so close, but she didn't. He ran down the alley and she followed him. Mr. Butts Cooper was in the alley and told her, "Don't kill him Carolyn, it ain't worth it."

Even though I never knew them as a couple. Even though I was aware that they weren't together because my dad had been physically abusive towards my mother. The little girl me still wanted them to be together and would be angry whenever someone else tried to have a relationship with my Momma. I didn't really understand how messed up it was that he wasn't an active participant in my life. The older I got, I knew I didn't want my mom to be with anybody else. I hoped that she and my dad would get back together. I just knew him as the guy in the white pickup truck that would sometimes give us money or a ride.

6. 12th Avenue - Age 8 and 9

THE FIRE

Chirp. Chirp. Chirp. It was the middle of the night and smoke filled the air. The smoke detector was going off and jerked us all out of our sleep. We jumped up and made our way to the yellow kitchen where the smoke was even heavier. The basement door was burned to a black crisp. Momma was already there by the time we got in the room.

Momma's life insurance broker had been encouraging her to get a renter's insurance policy for a while, and she had been putting it off and putting it off. She was struggling to keep up with payments on the life insurance. Sometimes she would avoid answering the door when he came to collect the monthly premiums or have us tell him she wasn't home. How would she be able to afford life insurance and renter's insurance? It wasn't until the insurance agent shared a story with her about one of his other clients that she decided it was worth it. There was a terrible fire at the clients home that destroyed everything. Thankfully, she was all paid up on her premiums so the insurance company paid her quickly for the damages.

We were struggling financially at the time of the fire. If Momma hadn't recently decided to get the renter's coverage, it could have been devastating. Momma was paid up on her rental coverage, so the insurance company wrote her a check for the damages. Luckily, the fire was isolated to the kitchen and the basement door, no other part of the house was damaged and none of us were hurt.

Floor heater we jumped over on 12th Ave.

Twelfth Street was my favorite house when I was younger. We always referred to it as West 12th Street but apparently, it was 12th Avenue. I have so many concrete memories from that house. The amount of space was more than any house we had before. There was white vinyl siding with scalloped awning around the carport on the side, a spacious living room with a beautiful picture window that took forever to clean but offered a view of the front yard, and the woods directly across the street. The front hallway had a large metal grate heater vent in the floor that we would leap over to get to the back bedrooms. There was a den in the center of the house that Momma converted into a bedroom for herself. There were 2 bedrooms in the back that you could only get to by walking through Momma's room; one for me and Brittany and the other for Mark. The front bedroom was for Fallon and Moria when she was around. The den had a beautiful fireplace that was perfect for hanging Christmas stockings on. There was a door in Momma's room that led outside to the carport. One night, Momma was sitting on the couch in her room. She could see out the window to the carport from the couch and happened to turn and see a man with long curly hair in her car. At first, she thought it was Jamal trying to sneak off in the car because he had long curly hair, but as she looked closer, she realized the man was white. The car had a bad starter, and it wouldn't start up the first time you tried but the guy didn't know that and couldn't get it going at first. Momma grabbed her gun and ran outside. The man finally got the car going and drove off. She shot out the back window, then ran inside and called the police to tell them someone was stealing her car. The 911 operator told her, "Ma'am your car isn't being stolen; it's being repossessed." With no car, she had no way to get to work or the younger kids to daycare, but thankfully Aunt Delilah drove from Edmonson County to Bowling Green an hour early every morning to pick Momma up so they could ride to work together. The daycare was at Turner Industries factory where Momma worked as the kitchen manager, so she killed two birds with one stone.

There were two bathrooms, the smaller one in the back hallway was in between the back bedrooms and had a simple stand-up shower with a glass door, a toilet, and sink. Once when Brittany and I were taking a shower and absolutely 100% not horse playing or doing anything crazy, out of nowhere the glass door just shattered. We screamed and Momma came and rescued us. Surprisingly neither of us had a single scratch or cut, but it scared us. The front bathroom was bigger and had the traditional tub and shower combo and a large mirror that covered the entire wall. That mirror would become extremely helpful to us during family game nights. There was a basement with wooden steps that you had to access through the kitchen. We didn't really use it. We had a huge back yard full of trees we could climb. The trees had tiny holes in them. I don't know if that was natural to the trees, caused by critters, or someone using them for target practice, but we climbed them anyway. Across the street were woods with this tiny lake and honeysuckle that grew wild close to the road. To get to the nectar we would pluck off the bud and then pull on the stem at the bottom of the flower or place the flower directly to our mouth and suck out the honey. It didn't taste nearly as sweet or delicious as I had imagined it would. We could take a shortcut through the field to get to the grocery store. When it would rain, Brittany and I would go outside in the front yard and wash our hair in the rain for fun. I don't know where the idea came from or what made us think washing our hair outside was a good idea.

I had my own room but usually slept in the den with Momma, thanks to all the ghost stories she and Moria had told us over the years, like how my Uncle Joe's dead father had come to their house and carried him out the backdoor in the snow in the middle of the night, or how they lived in a big beautiful house and one day when Momma was cleaning and the kids were playing on the stairs, an invisible person picked one of my siblings up and threw them down the staircase, or how Momma had been cussing one day—something her granny hated—when suddenly she felt a slap across her face, only her granny had been dead for years. Or the story of "Johnny," which was a sleepover favorite. Johnny's mother sent him to the store to buy liver for dinner, they were poor and instead of spending the little money they had, he stole livers from the graveyard. The story goes on with the voice of the dead man saying over and over again "Johnny I want my liver back, Johnny I'm at the front door." There was no way I was going to sleep in a room by myself. If I wasn't curled up in Momma's bed, I was cozied up with Fallon.

MERRY CHRISTMAS

Christmas tended to be a big deal in our family. The 12th Street house is where Fallon taught us **all** the Christmas carols including the "12 Days of Christmas," and how to sing in a round, all the songs from her school choir like, "Children Go Where I Send Thee," that was one of my favorites. One year we found our presents in the back of the station wagon. We walked into the backyard and at first glance in the windows it looked like a bunch of trash or newspaper circulars, but when we looked closer, we could see it was actually boxes and boxes of toys and stuff. We didn't dare investigate any further than peeking into the windows. We used to always get giant Christmas trees, Momma only wanted real trees, sometimes bought at the grocery store, sometimes "picked up" from the grocery store. That was, until we started getting fresh trees cut down from the woods. Mr. James was a soft spoken, chubby old man who wore glasses and a church hat. I'm sure he had a crush on Momma and would do whatever he could to win her over, including driving out to the country to cut down a Christmas tree. He would drive us out to some random woods—the name of which I don't know—to pick out a tree. Once we found the one we wanted, he would cut it down with an ax and tie it to the roof of his car, drive us back home, and put the tree up. It sounds very Hallmark movieish, except we didn't drink hot chocolate or warm cider in the cold with snow piled up all around us and more snow flying around our faces. Plus, the guy **did not** get the girl. I don't even think he stayed long enough to watch us decorate. There's one downside to real trees, they must be watered to keep them from dying or catching on fire. We always had one of those skirts that went around the base to hide the tree stand, water, and to catch all the needles. I loved the time spent decorating with colorful lights we had to untangle every year, sometimes finding bulbs that had lost their light and needed to be replaced, hanging delicate glass balls of various colors carefully and strategically on the branches, then squeezing the thin metal hooks together to secure them in place, along with handmade crocheted snow white ornaments of angels, bells, skates, and more starched crisp and clean to the heavens topped with an elegant angel wearing a cream and gold gown. At night we would sit mesmerized by the soft blinking lights and holiday music coming from a small box at the end of the string of lights. During the years of plenty, we would also gaze at the mountains of presents, a house of 7 to 10 people leads to tons of boxes and piles of discarded wrapping paper.

Some years, our house looked like a bad dream of Ebenezer Scrooge in *A Christmas Carol*. The living room was barren with no tree or decorations in sight. Even if we managed to get a tree, that didn't mean there would be anything underneath it. As Christmas got closer and closer with maybe a tree and maybe not, with not a wrapped gift to be found and no stockings hung by the chimney with care, the mood of the house would start to feel depressed and anxious, sparked mostly by Momma. As a single mother of seven children, with three or four living at home at the time, and as an aunt of many but with two living in the home, as well as three grandchildren, Momma had a lot of weight and responsibility on her shoulders. While we were living on 12th Street, my aunt Australia went to prison for about 3 years, so my cousins DonDon and Michael came

53

to live with us. My sister Moria was constantly gone from the house, leaving Momma to raise her three children at the time. As the grownup, now responsible for a household of my own, I can't begin to imagine trying to just maintain the monthly bills and feed and clothe all those kids. Add to that the expectation of gifts, expectation of a huge meal, and not being able to deliver must have been heartbreaking for her. All those expectations were established by Momma, she established traditions and the norms for the household. Unfortunately, her emotional state would rub off on us and make us sadder and more anxious than we might have been if we had known the truth (ain't no Santa). Most of my anxiety came from knowing that she was upset, that she was depressed,and how that was going to dictate the mood of the house. If we had talked about reasonable gift requests. If we had talked about or someone had taught Momma budgeting and saving, maybe things would have been different. But discussing bills and money wasn't something we ever did, even when our utilities were about to be cut off. Nowadays, people post tips like buying gift cards throughout the year, so you won't be stressed come December or a 52 weeks savings plan. These are great ideas in theory, right? But at the end of the day, you have to have extra funds to afford a gift card or to put in the savings account, and in our situation the extra just didn't exist. Hell, I'm surprised at the number of bountiful holidays we did have. I probably don't want to know how she managed to pull it off. Even when it wasn't a holiday, it seemed like she always tried to get anything we wanted. Mark owned every gaming system under the sun from SEGA to Nintendo's to PlayStation, somehow, she always managed to get it for him. She got a lot of our popular wish list items, Easy-Bake Oven, Skip It, Etch-A-Sketch, and one of my favorites would be Baby Alive. I wish the holidays weren't so commercialized and that we had focused on other aspects of the season. I do miss the childhood energy and excitement of the holidays. I miss the tired satisfaction on my mom's face after we happily tore through wrapping paper and devoured enough food to feed a small army. She legit still cooks holiday meals like the Salvation Army might send over extra guests.

I was introduced to Islam when I was around 12 or 13; I converted shortly after that. I remember the first year that Ramadan, the month of fasting, occurred during the holidays. We usually eat dinner by 2 p.m. but the sunset—which signals the time of breaking our fast—wasn't until around 5 p.m. I wasn't eating and my nephew Jared, who was still in elementary school, looked at me and said , "Can't you just eat now and make it up later this one time?" As a Muslim, I don't celebrate most American holidays, but I sometimes miss Christmas trees with all the sparkly lights and beautiful decorations, and carols. Now I get to celebrate Ramadan and Eid with string lights, decorations, and delicious meals, and occasionally piles of gifts for my family. I've got the cutest picture of my stepdaughter, sitting in front of a pile of gifts in her dress clothes, waiting to be able to open them after our community prayer. While I no longer celebrate Christmas, I love going home for Thanksgiving. Now me, my siblings, niece, and nephews are old enough to cover the cost of her always extra, always elaborate holiday meals with multiple meats, a half dozen sides, and a half a dozen desserts. This is when she is being conservativie. Every year, we give her a budget and assure her that she doesn't need to make so much, and she blatantly ignores us. Every year she swears it's her last year cooking, and we ignore her as we write out the grocery list or send her new cookware and appliances. The moral of the story, being together and enjoying a good meal is all that truly mattered.

As a stepmom, I'm much more excited by creating memorable experiences. From sitting around the house eating junk food and playing games to enjoying movie nights. I love creating traditions as well, like getting new pjs every Ramadan, Eid 1(Al Fitr), Eid 2 (Al-Adha), New Year's Eve, and birthdays. Don't get me wrong, I have spent way too much on piles of Eid gifts because there is just something fun about seeing your kid stare at all those presents trying to guess what they got, then watching them rip through wrapping paper that I end up cleaning up. But I love to sprinkle in experiences as well, like indoor skydiving or trips to amusement parks.

The house on 12th Street was a house for being together. We used to play countless board games like Clue, Monopoly, and my favorite Headbanz. So, this is probably a secret I've shared with only a few people, but my niece Brittany and I used to cheat at this game. We had the biggest mirror in the front bathroom that covered the entire wall above the sink. One time while playing, I got up to go use the bathroom and I think, or should I say I hope, it was a happy accident. I saw the reflection of the card in the mirror and was like **bam**, now I have the answer. After that, I guess my niece Brittany caught on and started doing the same thing. I wonder if my older siblings knew we were cheating and didn't care or thought we were too young to do that.

MORE BILLS THAN MONEY

The cost of living on 12th Street was the highest we ever had. TeTe always said that it was a summer house, i.e not a house meant to be lived in year-round. At times, we didn't have money for food, rent, and utilities. Moria discovered a way to get us food, even when we didn't have any money. She

56

had worked in fast food restaurants for years and knew how they operated. She would call or drive out to McDonald's, KFC, Long John's Silver; whatever restaurant she felt like getting food from and tell them that she had been there the day before and they had messed up her order. Every single time they would give her free food. They didn't ask for a receipt, they didn't ask for info on who had been working the day before, they just took her word and she would drive away with bags of food for all of us.

Momma made too much to qualify for food stamps despite all the mouths she had to feed, so when she couldn't think of anything else to do, she would bring home "leftovers" and provisions from her job. The rent was high, and the bills seemed to have doubled. When money got tight, we took turns having electricity and no gas or having gas and no electricity. We became experts at navigating life in the dark. We had life hacks before the Internet made them famous. No soap, use shampoo. If your gas is off in the winter this could be a major problem living in the South, winter can be brutal with temperatures in the teens and even single digits. Kentucky gets cold, cold like several feet of snow cold. I'm talking dress in layers cold; see your breath cold. My mom had a hack for that too, kerosene heaters that smell terrible but could efficiently heat a room. When we had to use the heaters, we would typically all sleep in one room, because we didn't have enough heaters to spread them throughout the house. I'm quite sure it was also easier for Momma to cautiously watch over one heater instead of many. I wonder if she slept at all or if she worried all night the house might burn down with one false move or issue with the kerosene heaters? When there were no heaters available, we would bundle up in layers and pile on multiple blankets, and sleep as many as we could in one bed for the extra body heat.

GATHERIN KINDLIN

Momma sent us kids into the backyard to gather kindlin, small pieces of wood we needed to add to the fireplace to fuel the fire. She was going to cook for us in her room. We didn't have any power, but we still needed to eat. Aunt Delilah wasn't a blood auntie, but she was Momma's best friend. They met working at Turner Industries where Momma was the head cook and kitchen manager, and Delilah worked alongside her. She was from the real country, Edmonson County, Kentucky. Her family lives down in the Holler which might not mean anything to you, if you're not from the country. They have tricks and ways of getting by we hadn't thought about. She taught Momma how to cook in the fireplace and it became a powerful tool in our life hacks toolbox. Gathering these little pieces of wood, watching Momma start a fire, and cook a meal all seemed like fun at the time. Now I can also recognize it as part of our effort to survive. You've got to be a great cook if you can make a meal without technology telling you when the stove has been preheated to the right temperature or a timer beeping to let you know it's finished. To be honest, I don't remember what we ate. It could have been something as simple as hot dogs and pork and beans. I just remember that experience of being in the backyard, looking for little sticks, and watching my mother make a fire in the fireplace. We were real *Little House on the Prairie*-ish. I don't think I would have survived, nor do I have the skills to cook like that. Now as an adult, the only time I cook over an open flame is when I'm roasting hot dogs or making s'mores with my stepdaughter. When we first got our fire pit, something I had wanted for years and years, I had no clue how to start the fire. I just remember telling my husband we don't have any trees in our yard, so I don't know how we're going to find anything to use as kindlin. Eventually, he got the fire going, but every time after that we decided to just use the easy starter logs. Using the fire pit is one of my daughter's favorite experiences. She legit said this is the best day ever or something along those lines. This is funny 'cause she's had a lot of fun experiences like traveling to Orlando and going to Universal Studios or indoor skydiving at iFly that cost me a lot more money. But the simple experience of using the firepit was the one she said was the best. Every year we look forward to the weather getting cool enough for us to light up the firepit again and break out the hotdogs and smores.

BORROWED POWER

One summer night, we were all laying around in Momma's bedroom with nothing to do but stare into the darkness. Out of nowhere she said, "Do y'all wanna watch TV?" which made absolutely no sense because our electricity was off **again**. But of course, without hesitation, we all said, "yeah," excitedly. Momma got up and left the room, and moments later when she returned, she clicked on the TV and bam cable. Never mind the logic of having cable but no electricity. We watched TV for a bit then fell asleep. For days after that, she would wait until dark, leave the room, return moments later, and turn on the TV for us to enjoy before bed. One night we all fell asleep with the TV still going. The next morning, she jumped up and rushed out of her room, through the kitchen, and out the backdoor to quickly unplug the multiple extension cords she had been running from our TV to the power outlet on the side of our neighbor's home. Mrs. Orr was a small elderly white woman with a bad hip, she used a walker or a cane to get around.

Momma developed a friendship with her over food and doing random favors like bringing in her mail, newspaper, or picking things up for her from the grocery store. She lived alone and besides Momma, the only visitor I ever saw was a Home Health Aide. We rarely saw Mrs. Orr, but anytime my mom cooked a big meal, she made sure she sent her a plate. Momma had been *borrowing* electricity from her without permission, and she was afraid that the Home Health Aide who came to work in the morning would see the extension cord and the jig would be up. This is definitely one of the less scrupulous, "lights off life hacks," that my mother came up with. I'm not endorsing it or recommending it by any means, just sharing our truth.

One cold and snow-stormy day, we needed a few things from the grocery store but as happened often, we didn't have a car. There was one store within walking distance in good weather, but it was quicker by bike. My cousin DonDon was the only one that had a bike, so Momma sent him to the store. He bundled up in his black bubble coat, matching toboggan, and gloves and rode off into the snow. We waited and waited for him to come back with the milk, bread, and whatever other odds and ends he had been sent after. After a while, Momma got worried and angry that he still hadn't returned, so she sent my brother Mark out to look for him. When I talked to DonDon recently, I asked if he remembered that ride in the snow? He said, "I made it to the store and bought the gallon of milk, the man in the store put it in a bag, and I wrapped the bag around the handlebars of my bike. The milk weighed more than me. I started riding the bike and it tipped over and I went down. I was stuck in the snow for at least 10 minutes. As my head arose from the freezing snow, I looked up and Mark was coming down the street like a lone cowboy coming to save me." He said that experience is why he hates

60

snow to this day. For me, it was just another example of us getting through tough times together and always having each other's back.

CHARGE IT

"Stick your hand in there, can you reach it?" Momma asked from behind me. I never went down into the basement, it was dark. I had small hands, so she figured I could reach the plastic credit card she had shoved into a hole next to the stairs. Movies and sitcoms used to show people using a chisel or hammer to retrieve a credit card they had frozen in a block of ice to stop them from using it. I guess Momma thought the freezer wasn't enough of a barrier to her swiping the credit card.

Blessing can come from anywhere, including the mailbox. The card just arrived one day. She hadn't applied for it but there it was, not one of those dummy cards with the name Jane Smith and random numbers on the front. This was a real card that had a real balance and real name on it, just not the name of anyone in our house. Momma started using the card slowly, not sure how credit cards worked or how it had arrived in our mailbox. She spent a little here and there. After a while, she got scared that someone would realize the card was being used, so she stuck it in the hole and waited. This little hide-and-seek happened at least twice. One of those times, she had my niece Brittany down in the basement sticking her hand in the hole. She spent roughly 7 grand. Then she waited for the cops, waited for trouble, waited for the coast to be clear. Some time went by and the temptation of the card just sitting there collecting dust was too much to resist. So, there we were in the basement with me reaching my hand into a hole, trying to feel around for a thin piece of plastic to pull out our secret blessing. In the end, she took $2500 in cash off the card and finally cut it up. According to Momma, that credit card was a miracle sent to her.

L.C. CURRY ELEMENTARY

One of the best things about living on 12th Avenue was our school, L.C. Curry Elementary. It was my first school. My cousin DonDon also went there and my Momma and his stepdad, True, took turns taking us back and forth to school. When we were in first grade, we happened to be assigned to Ms. Ragland's class. DonDon's dad had several adult kids from his wife who was not my auntie. In my youthful innocence, I remember telling her repeatedly that she was his sister and her getting upset with me because she did not acknowledge him as her brother. Our Principal, Mr. Cobb was a stout bald man who was the total **pal** in principal. He would read us stories during a weekly assembly, he also taught us random facts like if you have hiccups, you can eat peanut butter to stop them. L.C. Curry was also the school where I was introduced to Kids on the Block puppets. The puppets taught us about diversity and social issues like child abuse, bullying, and divorce. There were puppets from different racial groups, some with arm braces, and others in wheelchairs. The school even loaned out bikes to us on the weekends. We could go on Saturday and check them out for the weekend or a week at a time during the summer. For low-income families, it was probably the only way some of us would have had access to a bike at the time. I didn't know how to ride a bike, so for a while I had to borrow a bike that had training wheels on it. My family teased me endlessly, calling me *Training Wheels*

Trina because they are horrible. Once I learned how to ride without training wheels, I could borrow a big kid bike and we would ride around the neighborhood.

Fallon was like a little mom. As summer break came to an end, she would start putting us on a back-to-school schedule. For two weeks, she would send us to bed earlier to prepare us for having to wake up early for school. There were other things we needed to do in preparation for a new school year like back-to-school shopping. The same uncertainty that we felt during the Christmas holiday, we felt during the back-to-school rush. We didn't know if we would have new clothes or school supplies for the first day. Sometimes we were fortunate enough to get a week's worth of new clothes and new shoes, as well as our basic supplies. Then we would have to start wearing our old things and hope that Momma could get enough money together to add new items to our wardrobe throughout the year.

Field trips are a major part of elementary school, some free and some that require a fee to attend. A lot of times Momma couldn't afford the extra expense, so she would send me to school expecting that I would spend the day in class. On a few occasions, my teachers would call her at work to see if she had just forgotten to sign my permission slip. When she explained that she didn't have the money for me to go, my teachers would get verbal permission for me to go with my class. I guess they didn't want me to have to stay behind while the rest of the class was out having fun. I assume that those kind teachers were paying for me out of their own pocket. Other times, I would end up staying at school either in another teacher's class or in the gym. A few years ago, my stepdaughter had this really big field trip to the beach and an amusement park with her daycare. Her dad paid for the trip and she was so ecstatic that she told him, "Daddy I'm so glad

Allah made it possible for me to go on my trip because I really wanted to go." Her happiness at something so simple reminded me of how I felt when I was a kid and didn't think I could go on a trip and then a miracle would happen and my teacher would tell me that I could.

BLESSINGS IN THE WIND

Back in the day, people would either buy money orders or physically go to the utility companies and pay their bills in cash. I don't think Momma ever had a bank account. Sometimes she would send Fallon to the store with the money and a list of the bills that we needed money orders to pay. One afternoon, we were sitting in the car after going to pay the electric bill. We looked out the windshield and saw pieces of paper flying everywhere. The closer we looked, we realized it wasn't just random paper. Momma yelled, "Get the money, get the money," and we all jumped out of the car and started grabbing the money as much and as quickly as we could. We grabbed the last little bit from under the bushes and got back in the car. I don't remember anyone else being around and I don't remember the drive home. I just remember the pure adrenaline and excitement of rushing out of the car and grabbing bill after bill as they fluttered by in the wind and my Momma right beside me. Paying that bill left momma with just a few dollars to last until she would get paid again. It was a miracle for us to be there in that spot when suddenly the wind decided to send money in our direction.

EASTER-MY PEGGY

Easter was a treasure hunt in our house. Simply hiding dyed eggs in the yard wasn't enough for Momma. I don't remember ever having an Easter egg hunt at home. Store bought baskets with that terrible plastic green grass were just a base. She would add more candy and giant chocolate bunnies then hide them in random places throughout the house; in a cabinet, the oven, on top of the fridge, anywhere. One year, I found a basket in the dryer. She would also cook a nice big Sunday dinner that was ready by the time we got out of church. Momma doesn't believe in God, but she never prevented us from going if we wanted. She passed on her grandmother's rule that girls don't wear pants to church and must always wear stockings. Many a Sunday, we were running to the store to get a pair of stockings in the right shade, then pulling them on in the backseat because that was a rule she fully enforced. To this day, I never wear pants to the mosque, but I have abandoned the stockings rule. Easter was also about getting dressed up. Me, Brittany, and Fallon attended Little Zion Baptist Church over on 5th Street. My dad's office was right down the road. I believe my Aunt Regina was the one that first took us to the church. If Aunt Regina wasn't going, Mrs. Kathy or her sister Louise would take turns picking us up and taking us home. On special days like the pastor's anniversary or when other churches were visiting, they would have huge meals like fried chicken, dressing, deviled eggs, cake; the works. There is nothing like black aunties' and grannies' church food on a Sunday afternoon, after hours of sitting still in church. We would file downstairs to the kitchen in the basement, then line up as they served our plates. On regular Sunday's, we would walk over to the Save-A-Lot grocery store in between Sunday school and the main service. We would get Now and Later's and chips, soda, and whatever other junk we could sneak back into the service. Little Zion always had Easter egg hunts in the grassy area on the side of the church, some of the plastic eggs contained money. Easter Sunday was a time to dress your absolute best, usually in a new outfit. Picking out the perfect dress and shoes was one of the things we looked forward to. Momma had two friends named Peggy. Peggy Depp worked in restaurants like Momma and had kids around the same age as my brothers and sisters. The other was Peggy Cullum, but I just knew her as *my Peggy*. She worked in the medical field and was rarely around. Whenever Momma said Peggy was coming over, I would ask, "Which one, your Peggy, or my Peggy?" Both Peggy's loved on me and spent one-on-one time with me, but Peggy Cullum was *my Peggy*. She was known as *my Peggy* because whenever she popped by, she made sure to spend time with me, not just Momma. She loved to spoil me. She would take me shopping for new shoes at Shoe Carnival or to JC Penny to pick out my outfit for Easter along with frilly socks and shiny white shoes. I don't know why she took such a shine to me over everyone else in the house, maybe because I was the baby and was always under my Momma, but I loved when she would come around and spend time with just me. Once I graduated from Spalding, I remember shipping my nephews Easter baskets filled with candy and goodies and being so excited to spoil them. I only did it one year because that whole being Muslim thing, it's not a holiday we celebrate, but I wanted to relive that tradition through them.

NERVOUS BREAKDOWN

"I need help. I can't do this no more." Momma picked up one of her knickknacks and hurled it hard at the dark gold framed mirror on the wall. "Bang!" Little black marks formed on the otherwise spotless glass, freckling it forever. She was having a complete and utter nervous breakdown in the middle of the living room. She was screaming and crying out to no one in particular for help. Moments later, out of nowhere, my aunt Mary Jo pulled into the driveway in her white Cadillac. She has always driven Cadillac's. She and Momma started talking and she told her, "*Carol-line*, (in the way only Aunt Jo did) something told me to come here. I'm going to help you and your children." Aunt Jo worked at the Housing Authority of Bowling Green for years and was highly respected there. She told Momma she would help her get a house.

When they were young adults, Aunt Mary Jo had decided she wanted to go to the Job Corps to pursue a career in secretarial work. She had nothing that she needed to go off to the program, as far as clothes and luggage were concerned. At that time, Momma and some of her girlfriends would go around "boosting" so they got together and stole everything she needed to be presentable during the program. Once she successfully completed the program and was ready to get a job, they also boosted a full secretarial wardrobe so that she could look and feel the part. Momma believes that these actions in their young adult years are what made Aunt Mary Jo feel compelled to help her get a house in the projects, even though her history might otherwise prevent her from qualifying.

Aunt Jo is my Momma's oldest sister. She was married to Uncle Mitchell. She was a tall high yellow woman with dark freckles and always wore her hair and her wigs short. Momma said she was "built like a brick shit house back in the day." Those are her words not mine. Aunt Jo, on first impression, had an air of calm reserve, professional; but on occasion, like when she was playing cards with Momma and Aunt Bop, she would let an unexpected cuss word slip out. I never expected it but it always made me smile. Uncle Mitchell was tall, dark-skinned, and quieter than Aunt Jo. He just kind of glided through gatherings. She was the only person in our family I knew who had lived in the same place for as long as I could remember. When I was big enough to help, she would pay Momma and I to come over and help her clean the house on the weekend. She had two living rooms just like my grandmother used to have. Grandma and Aunt Jo had a thing for white furniture. The fancy living room had such beautiful, elegant furniture like a white chaise with cherrywood arms and legs that you weren't allowed to sit on. We could go in to clean, but any other time—like the occasional Sunday dinner—we could only admire the pieces from the door. The other living room is what we would today call the family room. It had a red brick fireplace with mantle, photos of her children, herself, and husband lined the top, as well as the surrounding wall. Accolades like college degrees and high school certificates and diplomas covered the wall. On the opposite wall was a long-oversized sofa and a matching loveseat. There was a window that looked out to the backyard where her dogs, Siberian Huskies, stood guard. She always sat in the recliner in front of the fireplace. After that unplanned Friday visit, Aunt Jo kept her word and by the following Monday, we packed up another U-Haul and moved one last time, to the projects.

7. 700 Gordon Avenue - Age 10 - 17

THE PROJECTS

We moved to the projects in September of 1995, right before my 10th birthday. I have always loved my birthday. I was one of those kids who would start counting down from January how many months and days (9 months and 10 days to be exact) I had until my birthday. We have a family tradition of getting our birthday cakes from Riley's Bakery. I don't think we knew of any other bakeries, well excluding the grocery store bakery. Riley's cakes are not cheap and when Momma didn't have the money for a cake from there, she would bake our cakes. One year, she made a beautiful, delicious chocolate cake—my favorite flavor—with fresh strawberries. The move took all of her money, but she still wanted to get me a Riley's cake, so she called Albert and told him that my birthday was coming up and that she needed money for my cake. He brought her the money and I got my bakery cake.

For years, Momma had spoken about never wanting to live in the projects. She never really said why, but her negative feelings rubbed off on me, causing me to feel apprehensive about the move. I think there is a degree of shame attached to living in government housing. That feeling of shame for needing help is also part of the reason in hindsight I think we struggled as much as we did over the years. Momma is a do-it-yourself kind of woman, working and hustling however she could. I think her ego prevented her from asking for help. I asked her recently why she was so opposed to moving to the projects. She said, "It was like giving up, once people move to the projects, they are usually stuck there. Just look at me." I guess she was right. For some people, moving there can cause them to get stuck. I'm 35 now, so she has been living there for 25 years, although she did move to a smaller unit in the projects after all the kids were grown. But not everyone allows moving to the projects to be their final stop. I know at least two families who moved out, including my friend Valentina and her family. They moved to the United States from Bosnia and lived in the projects for a few years. They moved into our same courtyard and then eventually bought a home in Whispering Hills, a nice subdivision in Bowling Green.

For about the first week or two after we had moved, Momma kept talking about making liver and onions. She really hyped up this meal, and I couldn't wait for her to cook it; she is an excellent cook. We love everything she makes. Every day I would ask her when she was going to make the liver and onions and every time we went to the store, I would ask her if she was going to get the stuff to make liver and onions. Then one day, I stopped and asked her, "Do I even like liver and onions?" She just started laughing and said, "I wondered when you were going to ask me that." Turns out I DO NOT like liver and onions.

The house was one of the biggest units available in the Projects, 5 bedrooms and 2 baths; one for the boys and one for the girls, and a large kitchen with space for a washer and dryer. With so many people in the house, we were constantly doing laundry. By "we," I mean the girls; Fallon, Brittany, and me. Moria was an adult by then and never lived with us on Gordon. She wasn't very stable; she moved from place to place, sometimes living on her own or with her friends in different houses and apartments in Bowling Green. Sometimes her kids would live with her, but they always ended up moving back in with us for the stability that Momma provided. She even moved to Fort Cambell, Tennessee, where she married her first husband Harold; he was a soldier. Their living situation was so bad that Brittany, who wasn't even that old, called Momma on the phone and told her, "Nanny, come get us." Derrick didn't live with us either, but he would sometimes drop off clothes to be washed and ironed. I loved doing his laundry because I would always find money in his pockets, good money too, like $20's, $50's and I think one year there was a $100 bill in his pocket. I found it while ironing his clothes for New Year's Eve. Apparently, he hadn't worn that outfit since the previous New Year's Eve. Keeping the house clean was something Momma took seriously. This was beyond those memes you see online of teary eyed kids holding cleaning supplies on Saturday morning with the greatest hits from the 80s and 90s playing in the background. The kitchen was not to be neglected. One night, I was sound asleep in my bed when Momma woke me up and told me to get in the kitchen. Brittany was in there too, looking just as dazed and confused as I was. We had made the mistake of going to bed without cleaning the kitchen first. She asked whose turn it was to clean. I said it was her turn and she claimed it was mine. She made us wash not just the dirty dishes left on the stove and in the sink, but we had to wash every single dish in the house, including clean ones minding their business safely in the cabinets. We had to wipe down the stove, the countertops, the kitchen table, and sweep the floor. The counters, stove, floor, and table were all a part of cleaning the kitchen every single night, and we were supposed to take turns washing or rinsing the dishes and sweeping the floor or wiping the counters. Of course, we always wanted to be the one who did the rinsing or wiping off because those were the easier jobs. And of course, we never agreed about whose turn it was to do what. Moria had told us about one time when she didn't wash the dishes and Momma woke her up in the middle of the night and made her wash every dish in the house, not just the dirty ones she had left in the sink. I didn't think she was being serious until she did the same to us.

Momma didn't really believe in boys cleaning. I would even clean Mark's bedroom, polishing his furniture and putting his clean laundry in his room. That was the only time anyone was allowed in his bedroom; he is a computer master and even had this creepy automated message that would randomly play on his computer that said, "Slade someone has entered your bedroom." At least I hope it was random and he didn't really have a way of telling when we opened his door. Boys were only required to take out the trash, clean the trash cans—which when they got really dirty and stinky included walking them down to the carwash—and maybe vacuuming.

TAXI

After we got the house in order, we had to fill it with food. The grocery store was right up the road. When we did big shopping trips, we would borrow a shopping cart and push it down the back street behind our court because there was no sidewalk on our side of the street. This was before they started putting sensors in carts to lock the wheels when the cart got too far from the store. We then had to walk it back, that job was usually left for Mark. Other times, Momma would call Mr. Granville to chauffeur us around. Mr. Granville was a skinny old black man that drove a yellow cab. He would pick us up and take us wherever we needed to go. If we had bills to pay, Momma would call Mr. Granville and he would drive Fallon and us kids around to the different companies and wait for us to go inside, pay, then drive us back home. Fallon was the unofficial treasurer of the house, buying money orders, paying the bills, and trying and failing to keep Momma on a budget so she could better manage the household expenses. When we did big grocery hauls around the first of the month, we would walk to the store, get all the groceries, then after we checked out or while Momma was in line, we would go to the front counter and ask to use the phone to call a taxi. When I was younger, I used to have to go to the eye doctor every Saturday for a type of therapy that was supposed to help strengthen my eyesight. I have horrible vision in my left eye and much better vision in my right eye. I would watch these little images on the machine of a house and click when I saw the red light; up, down, left, or right. Half the time I didn't even see the light, I would just click the button when I heard the sound I associated with the light. These regular visits were an attempt to force my left eye to get it's crap together. I was supposed to go every Saturday morning to Dr. Avery's Eye Care which was not close to our house. Sometimes Momma and I would get up early and walk, sometimes we would catch a ride from someone at the gas station, and sometimes Mr. Granville would take us; he would even let Momma pay later if she needed to.

FOUR QUARTERS

Living in the projects, there wasn't much to do. We did the usual things, like playing hide-and-seek, TAG, Red Light-Green Light, catching lightning bugs, and riding bikes when we had them. We even raced each other in the middle of the courtyard. I've always been pretty fast. We would line up like they do on TV, all official, and someone would yell, "On your mark, get set, go," and I'd propel up from a crouched position and take off down the road with my bare feet hitting the hot pavement. I guess that's a country Kentucky girl thing—running with my shoes off—that I still do today. There was one park across the street, but the highlight of summer was going to the Girls' Club.

There was always something to do there. We watched movies, made crafts, danced, and played in the gym. There was an elderly lady, Ms. Bea, who taught us how to crochet using a large plastic wheel. I made a scarf and hat. It was fun and nice spending time with her. That was the first and only time I crocheted anything. We also learned to cook and make treats, like these delicious peanut butter candies we would make with powdered sugar, peanut butter, and butter. You had to mix it all together, then roll them into individual balls, and refrigerate them. To be honest, I don't remember them telling us how much of each ingredient, but I do remember some of the candies not even making it to the fridge. You would melt butter and powdered sugar, roll them into balls, and place them in the fridge. That was a recipe we could easily make at home on our own. The Club was also a place we could go and get fed. Most of us were low-income kids and in the summer, we didn't have the school lunch or breakfast to depend on, mostly we ate standard sack lunches, chips, a sandwich, and a fruit with the occasional pizza party.

But all the action didn't take place in the giant gray building on Scott Way. Girls' Club gave us the opportunity to go out and experience things in the community. We were grouped based on our ages into different classrooms and had different activities we would do. My age group, 10–12-year old's, were going on a field trip to the mall. I wasn't old enough to work and had no money of my own. I went home and asked Momma for money for the trip which was the next day. Unsurprisingly, she didn't have it and told me to call my brother Derrick. He is 22 years older than me and is the definition of a big brother. Anytime we ever needed his help financially big or small, he had our backs. I called him and as usual he came through and dropped off $20.00 for me. I was so happy that I would be able to go on the trip and had already figured out how I would spend the money, a little for food at the food court and maybe something small. Mostly, I was excited to not have to go on the trip broke or be embarrassed that I couldn't buy anything. Hindsight tells me that probably most of the girls going didn't have any money to go on the trip and if they did it wasn't anything more than probably 20 or 25 bucks.

That night, Momma told me she was gonna take half of the money that my brother had given me, leaving me with just $10. I think she said she was going to use the rest to buy groceries. Inside I was so angry because she told me to ask Derrick for the money, he gave it to me for my trip, and now she was going to take half of it. It wasn't fair that she wanted to use it for other stuff. I went to bed angry and when I woke up the next morning, I was still upset. On my way out of the house, I saw the rest of the money lying on the kitchen table with a mix of bills and a bunch of change. She had counted out the money that was meant for me and stacked it up. I don't know what came over me, but I reached out and took four quarters.

I went to "The Club" feeling super anxious and mildly guilty. In my mind, I told myself it was rightfully my money, he had given it to me, but inside a part of me knew she took it for a good reason. I felt a little rebellious and mad. Selfish I know. But at that time and age, I think it's normal to be a little bit selfish and self-absorbed. I think the buildup of years of struggling and having to ask my brother only to have it taken got the best of me. I was thinking that my mom couldn't take care of things on her own and that she was taking my help from me.

My niece, Brittany and Derrick's girlfriend's daughter, Miosha had gone to Girls' Club with me and were both in their own classes when we got a call over the intercom to come to the front office. Instantly, my heart started racing and fear rushed in. I knew the jig was up. I knew that she knew. I was caught and trouble was coming. My first thought was to get rid of the evidence, so I turned to my friend and next door neighbor, Tina and said, "Here you want a dollar?" She of course said yes, and I handed her all four quarters. I walked to the office, and they told me that my mom was on the phone. I felt a little bit of relief because at least she wasn't there waiting for us. I picked up the receiver and my whole body felt hot with fear. Momma angrily asked if I had taken any of the money from the kitchen table? Of course, I couldn't tell the truth, so I said no. By then, Brittany and Miosha had come to the office, and I handed them the phone and they each in turn said no which I knew they would because I was the guilty one. We handed the phone back to the staff and listened as my mom asked if any of us had spent any money there. They said no, not that they were aware of. Unsatisfied with that, she ordered us all to come home.

Y'all that was one of the longest and shortest walks of my life. When we walked in the door, Momma greeted us with the belt. I honestly don't remember exactly what she said, but I remember all of us screaming and crying. I think she said something to the effect of stealing from the family and one of us letting the others get punished for something only one of us had done, or maybe that was my subconscious screaming at me or a bit of both. She beat us from the front of the house to the back, the whole time yelling and telling us how we better find them quarters. We walked around looking on the floor, in the couch cushions, behind doors, etc., for these quarters I knew weren't in the house, the quarters I had intentionally given away so that there would be no evidence. We kept looking and then suddenly, out of nowhere quarters started to appear on the floor. I only remember us finding three. I'd taken four but given all of them to my friend Tina before we came home, so I couldn't have replaced them. I don't know who was dropping the quarters; my Momma, an angel, my niece Brittany, or Miosha. At first, I assumed it was my mom just trying to end it all and get one of us to confess. If it was one of the girls, they must have also taken some money from the table without me knowing it. But in my heart at the time, I just assumed it was an angel trying to save me. I couldn't take it any longer, letting Brittany and Miosha get beat for something I had done. Finally, I confessed that it was me and Momma let them go and I got to endure several more licks. Then I was sent to my room for the rest of my punishment. I think I was supposed to be grounded for a week which meant no Girls' Club and no leaving the house. I cried myself to sleep. That evening Momma sent one of the girls to my room to ask me if I wanted to go to the store with them, which is the black Momma signal that, you're not totally still in trouble.

I asked my family recently and to this day everyone remembers the incident, but nobody knows where the quarters came from.

FOOD STAMPS

My childhood was tinged with some shame and embarrassment about our financial situation. Shame that we lived in government housing while I had friends who drove BMW SUVs to high school and lived in houses so big their parents had a stipulation in their contract that nobody could build a house smaller than theirs. I was also embarrassed that we needed government assistance to pay for basic things like food. Our food insecurity caused a lot of strain, but there was some relief in the form of multicolored pieces of paper. In the mid-90s, people still received paper food stamps in colorful booklets. Brown was used for $1 bills, blue for $5 and green for $10. We would try to be discrete when handing the multicolored bills to the cashier. But I'm sure people knew and were judging us on the first of the month as we filled our cart to the brim with meat, breakfast food, snack cakes, and drinks; along with other struggling families receiving food stamps. *In spite of* my embarrassment, it was a saving grace allowing us and so many others, to combat food insecurity and buy much more food more regularly thanks to this additional source of funds.

The financial strain was still there even after moving to the projects, despite the bills being much lower, we still didn't have much money. Momma is a brand name snob and if we ran out of Dawn dish soap, we would have to use the powdered Tide laundry soap to wash dishes. I hated using laundry soap, it made everything super slippery and while it makes your hands super soft, it is harder to rinse off the dishes and you have to use extremely hot water to dissolve it. If we ran out of body wash or soap, we would use shampoo to take a shower. Like most people, if we ran out of trash bags, we would use grocery bags and hook them on the drawer in the kitchen next to the sink. These were all temporary solutions. On occasion, Momma would have us take some food stamps to the gas station and buy inexpensive things like nickel candy or quarter candy and then get the cash change. Stores didn't have a way to give back food stamp coins so they would give us real money. We would each have to cash in several food stamp dollars to have enough to buy whatever non-food items we needed like dish soap, laundry soap, and occasionally Momma's Basic Lights 100s cigarettes, in the soft pack not the box. We got the benefit of getting a little treat for ourselves, as well as whatever household item we needed. Several years later the food stamp program changed from being paper booklets to a debit card. It made it easier to manage the funds and less socially awkward for shoppers to pay for goods, but we could no longer beat the system by buying low-cost items to get the change we needed to buy house-hold necessities and cigarettes.

We made a clubhouse in the shed behind the house. Momma had an old blue metal bingo machine collecting dust against the back wall from a business venture that didn't work out, but aside from that it was mostly empty. In the summer, we invited friends from the neighbor-hood over and we hung out eating treats bought with food stamps like snack cakes, potato chips, and drinking sodas and Kool-Aid. We went back and forth to each other's homes and played hide-and-seek outside until it got dark and the streetlights came on. We were one of the main hangout spots, since we had one of the bigger yards and we had a trampoline that everyone gravitated to, even kids who didn't live in our court. We would just find random kids outside jumping away like it was community property. I remember finding this little white boy who couldn't have been more than four or five, jumping one day and asking him what he was doing in our yard. He just looked at me and said his mom told him he could jump. Today, it's hilarious but at the time it was like, oh wow, that's bold to just show up to a stranger's home unannounced and uninvited. The trampoline was a factor in me converting to Islam. Momma used to leave her bedroom window open in the summer so she could hear us playing outside. One afternoon,4 we were sitting in her room watching Oprah or some daytime show, when we heard the familiar squeak of the trampoline springs. We went outside to see who was jumping and discovered some of the most handsome boys we had ever seen. I don't have the words to describe their complexion, but it was flawless tanned brown, but they weren't Hispanic, and they had shiny black hair; not too short and not too long. They were bouncing on the trampoline wearing tennis shoes and blue jeans. They told us their names were Elvis and Elvir and they were from Bosnia. We became fast friends with the whole family. I was infatuated with Elvir. He was at least 2 or 3 years older than me and was nice to look at. He barely spoke English, but he was a flirty young thing. His younger sister Valentina became my bestie and I spent lots of time at their house listening to music and eating food I had never had before. I loved that they were a real family with a mom and dad in the house. They worked hard and seemed to be so happy to be in Bowling Green. I learned that they were Muslim when I came over one day, and their dad Shaban, was leading a prayer circle and they explained how they were fasting for Ramadan. My infatuation with their family and especially Elvir sparked my curiosity in Islam, and I started studying the religion and even began fasting. Eventually their family moved to a different court in the projects once and then twice until finally they bought a home out in Whispering Hills Subdivision. They had been in America and in the projects for less than 10 years and they were able to escape the projects and buy a home of their own, something we didn't accomplish the whole time we lived there.

We had some fun times living on Gordon Avenue, like countless games of hide-and-seek and freeze tag, going swimming at T.C. Cherry pool, or going skating at the only rink in town. We also had fireworks wars on the 4th of July with the neighbors across the road. We shot off our biggest and best fireworks then they would shoot off theirs; on and on seeing who had gotten their hands on the coolest illegal fireworks. We had to drive all the way to Nashville, Tennessee to purchase ours. We are sure we won. At a certain point, our relationships with kids from two different families in the neighbors did a 180. Out of nowhere they started bullying us. They even had cousins who came to visit, and they added fuel to the fire, mostly out of jealousy. It was dumb and led to fighting on the block. It got so intense, the police were called and the management got involved. Our court was on a bit of a lockdown. There was no more neighborhood clubhouse, no hanging out in each other's homes, but at the end of the day we didn't really need outside friends. *In spite of* the neighbors turning against us, we weren't lonely, our house was full of people, and we had each other to lean on and we became closer because of the outside drama.

TO THINE OWN SELF BE TRUE

I remember it all very well looking back. For Reba, it was the summer she turned 18, but for me it was the summer of 6th grade. Actually, I don't remember it all very well, I remember it (my life) in bits and pieces, and I often remember it when a random song runs through my head or starts playing. Sometimes, I remember it differently than my family, but I guess that part is all about perspectives. The first time I heard the words to Reba McIntire's *Fancy* was at summer camp. My niece, Brittany, had been invited to attend Sheriff Jerry Peanut Gaines' Sheriff's Camp by her 4th grade teacher, Ms. Whittamore. Momma somehow got me invited to the camp as well. She probably wouldn't have let Brittany go alone. We rarely stayed overnight anywhere because Momma was always super protective. She wasn't one to really shield us from certain facts of life that other parents might have avoided. We knew the reason we didn't really do sleepovers was because she worried about who we would be around, who lived in the home, what kind of people they were, if there were men there, and if they were pedophiles or someone that might hurt us. If she didn't know them or couldn't ask around about them, we couldn't go. Plus, her standard of clean exceeded most people's, she never thought anyone else's home was clean enough. I'm surprised she let us go to an overnight camp, away from home, with strangers she had never met and couldn't ask around about, for several weeks.

They gave us a list of things to bring, like clothes, bathing suits, soaps and lotions, bedding, sleeping bags, and snacks. Momma somehow managed to get the stuff on the list, including plenty of Little Debbie cakes. The summer camp fed us of course, but it was nice having snacks that we probably wouldn't have been able to afford without food stamps.

I can't really remember what we did at the camp. I'm sure we did some crafts, slept in a huge cabin with a bunch of other girls, and interacted with the counselors. The thing I remember most was our camp counselor singing a country song I had never heard before. We were in our cabin and she was belting out this song and started teaching us the words. Momma likes different types of music, from Aretha Franklin to Anita Baker, from Blues music to Gospel and from Boy George and the Culture Club to Reba McIntire. We listened to everything, and I already loved Reba's music, but this new song *Fancy* became my favorite. At the time I had no idea she was singing about her Momma basically turning her into a call girl. All I knew was it was catchy. As I grew older, I could relate to the whole song. Her family was poor like us. They struggled to put food on the table, to pay the bills, and her daddy didn't stick around. At the end of the video for *Fancy*, Reba is wearing a fur coat standing in front of her old family home. She purchased the land and turned it into a home for runaway girls. ***In spite of*** her poor beginnings she found success. Her Momma did what she thought was best to make sure her kids survived, even if it was less than morally acceptable. My Momma never suggested for any of us to sell ourselves, but she has definitely done some things to survive that would be deemed less than socially or morally acceptable. When I was a teenager, I bought the CD with *Fancy* on it and now I can ask my Alexa to play *Fancy* and still sing along word for word.

LOSING AUSTRALIA

My aunt Australia moved to California in the mid 90s. Her husband had gone to prison, and she decided to relocate to San Diego where my Aunt Jo's daughter, Britta, lived. Australia was never afraid of anything and didn't hesitate to move across the country solo with just her two boys. Momma and the rest of the family were not excited for my aunt to be going so far on her own, and they also knew she wasn't the best driver. But cousin Britta had told the family all about her life there and how great opportunities were in San Diego, so that provided some comfort knowing she would hopefully have the support of family. My aunt got a great job working in food service at one of the stadiums there and she and the boys were doing great.

One night in 1997, I was laying in my bed trying to sleep and having no success. Momma was at BINGO and didn't usually get home until after 10 p.m. Someone came to the house and told us that my aunt Australia had died in a car accident. She had been out drinking the night before and had attempted to drive to work the next morning and was apparently still intoxicated. She did not survive her injuries. The whole family was devastated. That night I slept in Fallon's bed, something I did many nights when I was scared or had a bad dream. The strange thing is we didn't find out the same day that she passed away. It was several days later, before they were able to reach someone in Kentucky who could then inform Momma, but I think somehow that bad news I didn't even know was coming was what made it hard for me to sleep. Naturally, Momma took in her two boys DonDon and Meek. Neither of their dads were active in their lives and neither of them stepped up after they lost their mom. The day of her funeral in Bowling Green, we were all at our house afterwards when the lights went out on our block. Then for a while after that, whenever we would walk down to the corner store, the streetlight across the street from us would turn off when we walked by. I always thought this was a signal from my auntie that she was there.

At this point, Momma was raising her last three kids, her two nephews, and four grandkids all on her own. I have tremendous respect for that and even though she didn't always do the right thing, it was amazing that she chose to take on that responsibility. She could have easily let my cousins go into state custody as orphans. She could have allowed my sister's kids to go from pillar to post with her or tried to force her to come home and raise her own kids. She could have let them go into state custody as well but instead she owned that extra strain and committed to raising other people's children. There was some financial help from auntie's life insurance policy which Momma used to get things for the house and buy everyone clothes. At the time, we were all sad at the loss of my aunt but grateful for the ease the insurance money provided for some of our financial strain and being able to get a few things for ourselves. Today, I would say the money probably could and should have been used better but it was beneficial to everyone at the time including my cousins. It just might not have been the way my aunt would have wanted it to be used.

ANGEL TREE

Asking for help wasn't typically something Momma did. There were a lot of years when the Christmas spirit was dead in our house. It wasn't like it was a surprise event that popped up unannounced, it is the same time every single year but somehow, we managed to end up with no tree and no presents multiple times. Every year, we would make our wish list and hope for the best. One year, we received Christmas gifts from a prior year's wish list, things I had forgotten I wanted. The boxes didn't have tags on them, so we were all just opening each other's gifts. It turns out Momma had finally decided to sign us up for the Salvation Army Angel Tree and that's where all the gifts had come from and why there were no name tags on them. The angels buy and wrap the gifts, but they don't have the recipients names, so they couldn't fill out gift tags. The fact that she sat her pride aside and signed us up for the Angel Tree was a big deal. We probably should have signed up several other years, but it was a blessing we needed and surely a weight off her shoulders since she didn't have any outside help from our dads. Moria was sort of a rolling stone, so Momma raised her kids with little help from her and zero help from their dads. I believe this was the same year Aunt Jo gave each of us a gift. When I opened the wrapper and saw the writing and image on the box, I was a little bit disappointed. It appeared to be some type of back massager and of course I wanted to be thankful, but it wasn't something I really needed. Aunt Jo saw the look on my face and said, "Don't worry it's not what's on the box." Inside was a cute black corduroy jacket. I wore that jacket with everything.

THE POLAR REPORT

Our house was on the city/county line. Mark and Fallon went to Bowling Green High School, I on the other hand went to the county schools starting at Warren Elementary, then going to Henry Moss Middle School, and graduating from Warren Central High School. The county schools were prone to canceling school due to bad weather or even the threat of bad weather. Mark made a joke once that if they threw a piece of ice in the parking lot of Central, they would cancel school for the day. County schools had to contend with kids who lived up in the country on roads that were hard to travel down during icy or snow-covered conditions. City schools were filled with kids who lived in town and didn't face the same struggles making their way to school. Yet, we all watched the news at night during the winter when snow was expected. The Polar Report would crawl across the bottom of the screen, and we would hold our breath hoping to see our school, city, or county listed. Nine times out of ten Warren County, which my school was in, would pop on the screen, and I could happily stay up all night or later than usual knowing that I didn't have to go to school in the morning. One lucky night, however, the report showed not only Warren County Public Schools but also Bowling Green City Schools. There was a good reason that the city kids were finally getting a snow day. The next morning, we woke up to several feet of snow, making it impossible for any of us to make it to school or anywhere else.

We decided to go outside and play in the snow in the field behind our court. It seemed like every kid from the neighborhood was out there having the time of their lives. Mark decided we should build a snow fort using the red recycling containers to mold the snow into the shape of bricks. Our fort was so big we could walk around inside of it. I don't know how long it took us to complete this massive structure, but we were thoroughly pleased with our work. Unfortunately, some losers who must not have been from our court came by and decided to knock the entire thing down.

HOUCHENS MARKET-HOUCHENS KNOWS HOW

When I was a kid, I couldn't wait to get a job. Well, technically I couldn't wait to have my own money. I babysat here and there, but I couldn't get a real clock-in, paper check job until I turned 16. I turned 16 in September of 2001 but for some reason it didn't register that I was finally old enough to get a job until around February of 2002. I called the *Houchens Grocery Store* right up the street at Sugar Maple Square and asked if they were hiring. The manager, David Smith, told me I could come in for an interview in an hour. I left the house 10 minutes later. I was so excited for the chance to finally start making money. I walked in the door and asked for the manager, and he smiled and commented on the fact that I was early. David is a soft spoken and kind man, the type of person you would want for a manager. After a short interview, he told me I was hired and gave me the paper application to fill out. I went home thrilled. Because of my age, I could only work a few hours a day during the week after school and longer shifts on the weekends.

I would get off the bus and rush to the house. I was such a germaphobe that I never wanted to use the public restroom at school, so I would hold it as much as possible, then come running through the field behind our court and rush in the front door, throw my backpack on the ground or couch, and rush to the bathroom. Derrick used to always get after me about how bad it was to hold it in, especially after my niece Brittany was hospitalized with complete kidney failure and had to have a kidney transplant at 11 years old. Afterwards, I would change my clothes. I was happy to wear my red shirt and blue jeans and work the 3 or 4 hour shift. Sometimes I had enough time for a short nap before I had to trek the few minutes up the road to work. Some days ,I would be too tired and nearly in tears because I didn't feel like going. I remember Momma telling me to give her my shirt and she would go for me. That was hilarious.

Working at the grocery store was the perfect high school job. It was easy and we had some fun times. We gave out candy for Halloween and wore reindeer antlers or Santa hats at Christmas. It was mostly a bunch of high school kids and our middle-aged managers who were always in the office or in the back. We had couples form and fall in love and couples break up, we had invites to prom and the exchange of prom pictures, and we had seniors graduate and go off to college with the exchange of senior photos. We did have a few senior citizen cashiers who trained everyone, and retired while I was there. My favorite thing was when we were slow, and I could go and pull shelves. I would grab a grocery cart and step ladder and check the expiration dates on every box or bottled item then dump the expired stuff in the cart. Sometimes they would be a few months old, other times they would be years old and covered in dust. That whole first in first out rule doesn't always happen in grocery stores. Stockers just push the old stuff to the back and put the new stuff up front because it's faster and easier.

I trained most of the cashiers that started working there after me. One of the girls I trained was a bit of a dingbat. She was working on my cash register, and I was watching her and explaining how the register works, how to look up produce numbers, how to void an item if a customer changed their mind, and how to get cigarettes from behind the counter. She was finishing up an order for one customer when the next person in line told her they wanted cigarettes. She hit the button to cash out the order and turned to walk to the cigarettes which were in a case behind the customer service counter about 15 or 20 feet away. The register drawer popped open exposing all the cash in the drawer, and I yelled at her that she should never walk away like that leaving the drawer open so someone could take all the money out of my till and it would be me who would be accountable. Another girl I had trained had a much bigger problem with her register. She had been running the register alone for a while and this mistake is in no way a reflection of me as a trainer. A customer came in with a $100-dollar bill and asked for change. She counted out the smaller bills and handed it to them. The customer left the store and a few moments later the cashier turned bright red and started freaking out. We asked her what was wrong and she said, "The person that just left, I gave him his change and I just realized that I also gave him back the $100-dollar bill he wanted change for." We had to call the manager up front, and he had her shutdown her register and pull the till so she could count how much money she had to verify if she really did give him back the $100 bill. The poor girl was in tears standing at the customer service counter, counting her money, and apologizing. I think they took the money out of her check.

Our grocery store sold alcoholic beverages, but I wasn't old enough to buy or sell it. We had a few work-arounds that we used to allow customers to purchase alcohol from the mostly underage cashiers. Customers could scan the bottles or cases and we would scan all the other items. This was probably still illegal but someone in charge had decided this was an acceptable way to get around not having older employees on duty. Other times, when there were cashiers who were 18 or older, they would switch registers with us and finish up the transactions of customers choosing to buy alcohol.

The people I worked with were like my second family. Dottie and Ms. Joyce were the oldest cashiers, and they loved to work the morning shift at 6 a.m. On the rare occasions I was scheduled to work with them I would be dragging my behind and they were perky and alert, I don't know how. Well, Dottie wasn't perky, but she was alert. They were also the ones to train us new cashiers and who we relied on to run our registers when a customer was buying alcohol. It looked like a very boring square dance as we switched registers, us youngins would step out, the elders would slide in, and then we would go over and run their register while they finished checking out the customer. Ms. Joyce was sweet and friendly, all the cashiers and customers loved her, and Dottie smoked cigarettes out front on her break, had a bit of a grumpy exterior but she would help you and was nice once you got to know her.

5 FINGER DISCOUNT

Although *Houchen's Industry* is a corporation, Houchen's Market was a community store. The managers were always willing to extend a helping hand, including our family. Momma somehow arranged with the head manager, David, to get groceries on credit. He would let her charge the groceries she needed and then pay for them when she got paid. I don't know if it was her rapport with people, the appeal of a mother in need, the fact that she was a regular customer with a job, or if David's big heart made him take the risk and trust her to pay later. I don't know if any other manager, at any other store, would have been willing to do the same if Momma had asked.

One day, I was working on the register when one of the bag boys came up front and said that Roger had caught someone shoplifting. The lady had gone into the bathroom with black garbage bags and was putting food and personal care items like shampoo in the bags. I don't remember the police coming to the store. I believe he ended up letting her go home. Seeing his compassion for that customer

92

made me think about the times in the past when my mom shoplifted food. Sometimes she had the money to pay for it but didn't because shoplifting was a habit. Sometimes she didn't have the money and was trying to do whatever she could to feed us. She used to tell us the story about getting caught shoplifting from a different *Houchen's Market*. We lived on Fair Street and she was shopping with us younger kids. She had filled her cart with about $200 worth of food and her pocketbook with about $100 worth of meat. She has always carried large purses. The store manager came up and told her that he saw her stealing. At first, she said, "Oh my babies must have stuck that in there," and he replied, "Well they must be used to seeing you stick stuff in there." Then she told him, "I don't know why I did that; I have money, can I just pay for it?" She had about $600 in cash and food stamps in her purse. He told her no, and she asked, "Will you please let me send my kids home in a cab before you call the police?" and he let her. The police took her to jail but then the store called and said they weren't pressing charges, so she got to go home.

WHAT HAPPENS IN THIS HOUSE STAYS IN THIS HOUSE!!

There's a subtle difference in the aura of a house when the electricity is turned off. Maybe it's the lack of protons and neutrons running through the wires and the missing low frequency hum that appliances make. By the time we moved to the projects, we had become experts at navigating life without power. We had life hacks before the Internet made them famous. Want to know how to get your homework done with no power? Sit outside on the front porch and do everything you can before it gets dark. Do work on the bus

93

ride home. Want to know how to prepare for school in the early morning while it's still dark out? Select your outfit the day before when there's still some sunlight, lay everything you need in one location along with your backpack and shoes so you can find it fumbling around in the dark or by candlelight. Want to know what to do when you've run out of lotion? Use Crisco which doesn't have the most pleasant smell or Blue Magic hair grease, they work in a pinch. All out of maxi pads, you can use folded up old wash rags. Need to take a bath but the gas is off? Boil water in a pot on the stove, then carry it to the bathroom and pour it in the sink to enjoy a quick "whore's bath." In the summertime, if you are brave enough you can take a very brisk shower. First you let the water run for a little while so it can get close to room temperature. Then you get in and get wet, stand back from the water and soap up, then stand back under the stream of water and do a quick rinse off. There is no lingering; this is more army wash than luxury steam shower. *In spite of* the sometimes inconvenient living conditions, we made do, we were clean, we were loved, and we were safe.

Our family had a motto, actually my mother had a motto, "What happens in this house, stays in this house." It was usually easy to maintain the secrecy of our broke-ness from the rest of the world, but by the time I was in high school, it was harder to keep the outsiders at a distance. I was dating a true outsider my senior year. Anthony was from Chicago. He was short like me, wore glasses, and kept his hair in braids. He was sweet and there was something crazy about how my body reacted when he was anywhere close to me. Like a jolt of warm energy rushed through me that I didn't understand. It felt scary and good. It didn't happen all the time; it was random. I felt that feeling out of nowhere one day when I was working on the register at *Houchens.* The jolt hit me, and when I turned around, he was there standing behind me. He lived in the projects too and we would ride the bus home together. One day he got off the bus at my stop and walked me home through the back field. When we got to the front porch, I knew instantly something was wrong. The energy of the house was somehow different, no not different, it was missing. There was no energy because the power was turned off. Inside I tensed up in an almost fight or flight mode. I was embarrassed and angry that we were still dealing with this same crap. It wasn't my fault, and I couldn't control it and I hated that it was out of my control. I hated that we had no heads up that we would be coming home to darkness. We never had a heads up. I didn't want him to know how raggedy we were. It wasn't enough to be poor and living in the projects, we couldn't even keep the lights on. I was embarrassed that I couldn't invite him inside and too embarrassed to tell him why. I had never talked to anyone about our struggles because "what happens in this house stays in this house." I didn't tell my best friend and I couldn't tell him, so I had to think fast. I couldn't let him come inside. I don't remember what excuse I made. I think I said something about needing to get ready for work, but whatever it was I got him out of there fast and slipped in the door, into the powerlessness and frustration.

MY MONEY IS NOT YOUR MONEY

Minimum wage was $5.15 in 2002 and I was only part-time. I remember getting my first check and being shocked. It could use some of Popeye's spinach. Nobody bothered to tell me they were going to take out taxes. However, I did make enough to be able to buy my own stuff, like school clothes and whatever little snacks I wanted like 2-liter bottles of Orange Sunkist. I would get so mad when I would buy these big bottles of soda, go to work or school, and then come home to a nearly empty or missing bottle. I guess it isn't so surprising with a house full of people. Nobody respected the idea of having our own things. Fallon had given me her old prepaid cell phone. The only game on there was Snake which I was terrible at. I could afford to buy $10 or $20 reloadable phone cards. The minutes never lasted long, but this was back when you could tell people to call you after 9 p.m. when minutes were free.

I would occasionally order pizza for myself from Papa Johns. I would give Momma the money to pay for it while I was in the shower. She had the audacity to tip the pizza delivery person generously with my little monies, and I was so mad because I didn't feel like I could afford to be tipping anybody. Today it's hilarious because I'm a much better tipper, but it shows the level of broke-ness I had at my first job. I remember in my senior year of high school coming home from work and ordering a pizza for lunch. I left the money on the kitchen table and decided to take a quick shower. There were a few people at the house, including a family member who has struggled with drug addiction for years. I would usually be extremely cautious about where I left my purse when that person was around. I would keep it in my bedroom in a closet or a drawer but never just out in the open. For whatever reason, I was in a rush and made a rookie mistake. When I came out of the shower, the pizza driver was knocking on the door. I went into the kitchen to grab the money to pay them and there was nothing there. I knew immediately that I had got, got.

People in my family have struggled with addictions of all kinds from drugs and alcohol to gambling. The worst part of addiction is that it doesn't just hurt the addict, it spills onto the people they know and love and that love them. One of the ways it dripped onto me was when my Momma decided I should give her money. We had all tried to talk to her about her gambling in the past, but she didn't feel like it was an issue. I can't remember the amount she asked for, I think it was just enough to go to BINGO. I told her no and that wasn't something she wanted to hear. I had spent years being frustrated with the fact that she was receiving child support for me from my dad, and I didn't see a penny of it. He was supposed to pay $100 a week which he could afford as a very respected and active contractor. As a 'screw you' to her he would only pay $50 per week on the weeks that he actually paid. I didn't get to use it for things I needed, like clothes for school or for minutes on my phone. It just went in with the rest of the household money. Today I can understand it wasn't a lot of money, and I can maybe even rationalize that his little $50 was my portion of the household bills and $200 total a month doesn't go far. I'm not sure why she felt entitled to my money. Maybe in her mind, I should be contributing to the household since I was working. She had requested money from Fallon when she first started working, which caused conflict between them. I wouldn't relent, so she told me "If you don't want to give me the money, you can leave." This was one of the rare times when Moria was living in Bowling Green, so I went to stay with her. Somehow my dad heard about all the drama and gave me a call. I tried to explain to him what happened—at least my side of things—and he sympathized with me and just said, "Well you know that's how your Momma is about money." He didn't offer any type of advice and didn't invite me to stay with him, which would be the natural reaction if he had been an active parent. Eventually, Momma called Moria and told her I could come home, which I did. Then we awkwardly pretended like nothing happened, something that our family excels at.

This incident wasn't the first time someone in the family felt like they had a right to my money. I have always slept with my bedroom door closed. One night, I was in bed sleeping with my head facing the door, when light from the hallway filtered into the room falling on my small white metal vanity table. I would sometimes keep my purse there or on the back of the doorknob. I saw someone holding my purse, they saw me seeing them. Without saying a word, they put the purse down and slowly closed the door. We never spoke about it, and I never said anything to anyone else. I just felt really hurt because I knew what they were trying to do. After that, I started locking my bedroom door at night. During the day if I wasn't in my room, I hid my purse. I would put it on the top shelf at the very back of my closet or hide it in my waterbed. Mark and I had the same waterbeds. His was a dark brown and mine was a light oak. It was a super single length with a bookcase on the top and had a base made of 6 dresser drawers and at the very end was two doors that made storage space or cabinet. I rotated storing my purse between the closet and the hidden cabinet.

LADY LUCK

*Left: My Uncle Dougie Bowman and Center
My mother Carolyn Carpenter*

Momma is the best cook I know and working in food service as a cook or kitchen manager was how she made a living. She had a few other activities she did for fun, and to bring in extra cash that was less stable, like playing the lottery, BINGO, and poker. She won some and she lost some but as most folks know with games of chance, you lose way more than you win. My Uncle Dougie opened a *Good Time House* down on 3rd Street where people could come to play poker and shoot dice. He sold food and drinks as well, it was a 'popping under the radar' spot. We would go and visit him there but only in the daylight when there were no customers there. He had pictures of his friends and his customers covering the walls. He would give us cokes and chips while he and Momma talked. She spent a lot of nights there playing cards and helping run the tables, which earned her a cut of the money pot. Sometimes she would go to BINGO at night from 6 p.m to 9 p.m., then afterwards go play poker late into the night. Winning at BINGO or poker led to playing large amounts of money on lottery tickets from *Pick 3* and *Pick 4* to the *Powerball, Mega Millions,* and *Cash Ball.* Over the years she has played them all and won small amounts and large amounts. The problem however, was that there was never an end to some sort of gambling. Big wins were not enough and portions of her winnings always went back to playing numbers, to the BINGO parlor, or poker table the next day. When she wasn't going to play down at the *Good Time House* or *The Bottoms,* another place for illegal gambling, she would play cards at home with her friend Trey. He was an obnoxious, loud, country white man from Adairville, Kentucky. His family had money, which he blew and stole for gambling and other vices. They would be up late at night playing poker, Dad, or Bella while we were in our rooms trying to sleep for school the next day. Nobody liked Trey but Momma. Thankfully, he didn't stay in town long, since he worked in another city, but when he was in town they would gamble together.

In Islam gambling is consider a sin.

> *They ask you about wine and gambling. Say: 'In them both lies grave sin, though some benefit, to mankind. But their sin is more grave than their benefit.— Qur'an 2:219*[4]

Seeing how it affected our family, I understand why. We never really got ahead no matter how big the win. Eventually, my siblings and I decided that enough was enough and we had to get Momma to stop gambling. We somehow heard about Gamblers Anonymous and tried to do an unofficial intervention. We told her we felt like she had a problem and needed to get help. She told us that she enjoyed it and she didn't have a problem and had no plans to stop. She taught those of us that were interested how to play poker. It was fun using pennies, rice, or beans like money. I even won some. She let Fallon and I go to BINGO with her and secretly play a little before we were legally old enough to gamble. All the folks that run the BINGO parlors knew her and didn't say a word. I completely get the thrill and fun of playing and winning, but the gambling was doing more harm than good since the bills weren't getting paid and we didn't always have the basic things we needed. To this day, she still plays BINGO and lottery on a regular basis. Sometimes I call her when I have an interesting dream and let her interpret it for any potential numbers, or if I see a pattern or a number significant to me, I share it with her and she plays it. She still wins at both, but she gave up poker years ago.

ADDICTION

Gambling to Momma was a way to make money and to flip her meager earnings. But fast money usually ain't good money. Her regular 9-5 had us struggling to get by. But poker, lotto and BINGO weren't the only ways she tried to double her dollars, she also dabbled indirectly in street pharmaceuticals. Hustling narcotics has always existed in BG and several members of my family had played the game and lost time and time again, serving years in prison off and on. Momma thought it would be a good idea to try her hand at it by using one of my uncles as the corner man. He would be out in the street doing the deals, and she would front the money. He knew who the crackheads were in town because he was an addict. He along with two of my aunts and one of my brothers had all struggled with addiction to crack cocaine for years. They would use then stop, be good for years and on the straight and narrow then fall off the wagon and start using again. Bowling Green is so small and word always spreads back to the family of any misdeeds any of them get into or if they start buying drugs again. Their addiction was strong back in the day and caused some of them to do things that hurt the family. You see it on TV or in the movies, addicts not being able to care for their children or others robbing their own families, usually something like a few dollars from a purse, or stolen electronics. I know first-hand that it really does happen and shared blood isn't always strong enough to stop an addict from doing whatever they can to feed their habits. Two of my brothers were robbed, I lost chump change that I naively left on the table, and even Momma had money stolen out of her dresser drawer. All of us got, got by the same family members because that's how strong the addiction had them in its grip. It was winter when she decided to venture into business with my uncle as the man on the street. He was always wearing this big black and yellow bubble coat. My brother Derrick said he looked like a bumble bee. When he was using drugs, Derrick would call unc the Ghost of Gordon cause he would just be all over the place. One day Momma came in and told us she couldn't find unc and that he hadn't paid her the money for the product she had given him. She was worried about what he might have done, so she got in the car and went looking for him down on 3rd Street near Uncle Dougie's *Good*

Time House. When she finally found him, he was standing there in the middle of the street in his big black and yellow bubble coat looking guilty. She yanked him up and asked him where her money was or her product and all he could say was "I smoked it." Momma was pissed that she was out all that money and pissed at herself for thinking an addict would be able to control himself around all that dope.

COLLEGE BOUND

I was taking a shower when the mail came. It was my senior year at Warren Central High School, and I had already been offered a full-ride scholarship to Western Kentucky University. It was nice being wanted by my hometown school, but I had plans of getting out of our small town. My guidance counselor explained that with my ACT score of 23 I could get into any school in the state, so I applied to a few other schools and was intently waiting to hear from those in other cities. When I opened the bathroom door, I saw my mother holding a white envelope with yellow and blue letters. She looked at me guiltily and sheepishly said, "I was going to throw it away." I grabbed the envelope and was greeted with an acceptance letter from Spalding University in Louisville, Kentucky. I didn't know much about the school except it wasn't in BG and they wanted me. I wasn't the only one of my friends going away for college. Several were going to the University of Louisville and others went to schools in Kentucky but different cities. One night I was standing in the hallway between my room and Mark's talking about the trip to Freshman Orientation weekend and getting ready for the move to Louisville when he said, "You'll be back in a month." It was an off-the-cuff comment; I'm not sure he even meant it. I don't know if he said it because it was just something to say, if it was because I had never really been away from home, if he realized lots of kids go off to college only to end up coming back, or if he was trying to do some reverse psychology to trick me into not running away from home. When I asked him if he remembered telling me that years after I had graduated, he said he didn't remember saying it or know why he had said it. He sounded like he felt bad about it, but I'm kind of glad he said it. Maybe if he hadn't said it, I wouldn't have stubbornly tried to prove him wrong. Whatever his reason, his words stuck with me.

Houchens really came through for me my senior year. I was able to purchase my senior photos and yearbook. Spalding had sent us a list of all the things we would need as freshmen preparing to stay in the dorms. I didn't even think of asking anyone for help, I just started purchasing items off the list every time I got paid. I believe my Aunt Jo volunteered to buy my mini fridge or my microwave as a graduation present. I bought the hottest dark blue star-themed sheets, shower shoes, and a beige canvas laundry hamper that was made of like 20 pieces of black metal bars and had wheels I attached at the bottom so I could roll it to the laundry room. That stupid hamper fell apart numerous times. My aunt Diddy Bop's mom gave me a mini rolling suitcase as a graduation gift that I still use to this day. After I graduated from high school and went off to college, I kept working at *Houchens* every time I came home for holiday breaks or the one-week break in-between the six-weeks sessions at Spalding, I would call the manager David and he would let me work while I was home. I was so sad the day I found out he was going to be transferring to another store. David had given me my first job and had been so caring and compassionate to Momma when she didn't always have the money to pay for food, and I didn't like the idea of someone else taking on his role at the store.

8. Daddy Issues

Despite hearing for years that my dad's abuse was the reason behind my parent's breakup, deep down inside I still wanted them to be together. While my mind could imagine the abuse suffered at the hands of my grandmother (and used it to fuel dislike), it was much harder to picture the abuse my dad had inflicted. I had heard stories like how once Momma was wearing a halter top that didn't require a bra, Albert came up and scratched his nails down her breast and told her, "I oughta take it off you since you want to show off." Her breast swelled so bad she had to wear a sling. Or how he became abusive when she was giving him a ride home in her station wagon and she had a baby in the backseat. Momma was trying to be nice. She didn't even know they were still beefin. "I didn't know we were still mad." Out of nowhere Albert reached over and hit her in the face. Her friend Drake was driving and saw the car rolling down the road and Momma's head leaned over because she had passed out. So, he positioned his car so her car would hit his and stop. Afterwards he pulled her from the car and ran down the road and took her to her Momma's house. The lady that was in the car with him grabbed the baby and took the baby to her Momma's house as well. Her eye became so swollen, it looked like it was going to pop out. At that point, my grandmother gave her a gun and told her she had to protect herself. A few weeks later—after she healed up—she went to the neighborhood he lived in with his Aunt E and waited for him to come home. They were doing construction, so she hid in the construction area and as he got out of the car and started stretching, she shot him in the ass, and he took off running down the road. Shooting him in the ass was a story we always laughed at, but I never really pictured it.

I never saw the abuse for myself. The closest I got to domestic violence as a kid was going to a meeting at BRASS (Barren River Area Safe Space) with Moria. We sat and ate snacks and drank lemonade while the women sat in folding chairs in a circle and talked. I don't know what relationship she was in, but I didn't realize we were there because she was dealing with abuse. I don't think I heard the phrase "domestic violence" until I started working at a domestic violence shelter in college.

In my head because my father chose not to be a part of my life growing up, meant **he** chose not to be with my mom. I naively gave all the power to my dad. However, the truth is, my mother chose not to be with him. She was strong enough to fight back and she was strong enough to say enough was enough. I'm still trying to accept that even as I write this chapter. I get that we all have power in relationships, but in my experience, it just seems like men have more of the power. I always thought something else must have caused him to not want to be there. I never thought that I had done anything wrong or that it was somehow my fault, probably because he was never there, so I didn't lose him after having him in my life like a child of divorce. But I also couldn't understand why he didn't try to be in my life. The only answer he ever gave me was that he didn't get involved because of his issues with my mother. We are two separate individuals, and he chose not to be a father to me out of hatred for her or wanting to somehow punish her for choosing not to be with him.

Not fully accepting the reality of why their breakup happened, prevented me from fully expressing myself in my own relationships. Being from a single parent home created a slight but constant fear of saying or doing the wrong thing and being the cause of the end of my relationship. I guess my real daddy issue is one of abandonment. Relationships are fragile and conditional. My husband told me once that he was reading an article on how to love someone with anxiety. Much of my anxiety comes from the uncertainty of relationships and the fact that just as easy as it is for someone to choose to be with you, they can also choose to not be with you.

CONNECTION

As a kid I was my Momma's shadow. But despite how close we were when I was young, I was unexplainably obsessed with my dad or the idea of my dad. I wanted a connection to him. Like when I decided I was going to start using his last name. I even filled out an order form for CDs from BGM Music as Mary Hayes, you might remember those envelopes that came in the mail. Get so many CDs for 1 cent and then the rest you pay full price. Did anybody ever actually pay for those things? Yes, I know it's extra crazy that I used Mary on the order form. Mary Hayes probably owes the folks at BGM Music some money. I think because I didn't have much firsthand experience with him, I looked for anything to solidify our relationship. In some ways, I also elevated his importance and idealized a man I didn't know for myself. I don't know how Momma felt about me using his last name for that short time that it lasted. It wasn't something we openly discussed. I'm sure she was probably bothered by it, but she never sat down and talked to me about how I felt about my relationship or lack thereof with my dad. Whenever she talked about him, it was mostly out of anger and hatred. Sometimes her anger with me would be tangled in her anger with him. Her sharp tongue was reflective of the verbal abuse she experienced from her own mother Mary Elizabeth. I wonder if she could hear her mother's voice calling her a "*little black bitch*" when she would tell me, "*You're just like your black daddy.*" It was rare for her to speak to me that way because at the end of the day I was her favorite, her little chocolate drop. She used to say that she always wanted a little girl that looked just like her and then she had me. It was only when I displeased her or wouldn't do what she wanted that she compared me in that negative way to my father. Most days she spoke highly of all her children and instilled in us girls the phrase, "You are worth your weight in gold."

But when it comes to Albert Hayes, there is no mercy or sympathy for him with her. He doesn't deserve our love or caring because he wasn't there for us as a dad should be. Even to this day, it's like a competition in her mind between the two of them. Just recently, she asked if he were having a holiday dinner at his house and she was having one at her house, who would we choose. I don't know how she can doubt that she would win again and again when it comes to her role and importance in our lives. I don't know if she ever tried to foster or encourage a relationship between my dad and I don't think she felt it was important. According to her, I was the only one that expressed any interest in having a dad. It makes me wonder if she could have done something or said something to make him want to try to spend time with me. I don't remember him ever trying to come over and spend time with us and her turning him away. I just don't remember him making any effort. I know there were times when Mark would go and work with my dad in the summer on his construction projects to earn his own money. Maybe because I was a girl, he didn't know how to relate to me. I didn't have any solid interactions with him until middle school. Albert lived in a house within walking distance of us. He was living with Ms. Jackie, her daughter Whitney, and my two half-brothers Little Al and Dillon. I didn't even know that these brothers existed until we moved to the projects. Momma was dating this guy George, who annoyed the mess out of me. I didn't think he was very smart, I didn't think he was very handsome, and I just didn't think he was someone my mom should even be entertaining. I called him George of the Jungle. Whenever he would come over to see Momma, I would announce that I was going to my dad's. Poor George tried to win me over and even gave me money to buy my prom dress senior year. He was a nice man, but I had no interest in him or any other man trying to be with my mother.

I started babysitting for Jackie, watching my little brothers and their older sister. It was kinda strange being in a house that my dad lived in with his other family. And if I'm being honest, there was probably some unrecognized and definitely unverbalized envy. Mind you, I enjoyed being the big sister to my little brothers, even when they were annoying. But I was also dealing with the fact that they got to be with him all the time. They were all in the same home, whereas I had never had the experience of living with him. There was some curiosity of course, like what is he like. Does he read bedtime stories; does he play with them when he comes in from work? Who is he as a dad 'cause I never knew? One day when I was babysitting, we were all outside in the front yard and Dillon did something to annoy me, so I took the water hose and sprayed him. He was a snitch and said, "I'm going to tell Big Al on you," which is what they called my dad. And I just laughed and told him, "Your dad can't whoop me." My dad had never whooped me or disciplined me in any way because he wasn't around. I don't know if he is a tough disciplinarian or a cupcake who just caves when his kids are misbehaving.

Sometimes, I would just go to their house and sit on the couch with him and do mundane things like try to take a nap, anything to spend more time with my dad. I don't remember a single thing we talked about, I just remember wanting to be around him. Sometimes we would drive around in his truck and he would take me places like to have breakfast at a very popular hometown restaurant called *Teresa's*. He knows everybody and would introduce me to his friends. I always felt excited to be with him in public, excited that he wanted me around. But our relationship didn't really progress even though I had started spending time with him and I was there babysitting my brothers. It didn't lead to anything with depth.

As a preteen and teen, I was always the one making the effort to call or go see him. Even though my dad had his own business, made decent money, and was well respected for his professional abilities; he fell short as a father. He was ordered to pay $100 a week in child support. Every week Momma and I would drive to his office on 5th Street to pick up the check. It was a yellow check always written out for $50. I'm sure he could afford to pay the ordered amount, otherwise the court wouldn't have set that amount to begin with, but it was another way for him to stick it to my mom and do what he wanted. Despite all that, I tried to be optimistic. One year, I even called to wish him a Happy Father's Day which made Momma angry. I remember going in the other room to make the call and when I was done, she said, "I know you ain't call and tell that (insert some curse word) a Happy Father's Day." In hindsight, I agree he didn't deserve it but something made me do it. I don't remember him making any effort. She never tried to foster or encourage a relationship between the two of us. I wonder if she could have said or done something to make him want to spend time with me. She had no relationship with her own father so maybe that's why she saw it as unnecessary, but it was important to me at the time.

Once I started high school, I gave up on the idea of there being a relationship. I had other things to focus on like schoolwork, friends, getting a job, and making my own money. Our interactions were reduced to financial transactions. I would call him sporadically and ask for money. I used to participate in every school fundraiser, ordering a bunch of stuff like chocolate candies and those summer smoked sausages and cheese, Christmas wrapping paper, and just a bunch of unnecessary things. We couldn't afford it; I don't know what in my brain made me keep thinking, *I'm gonna order this stuff and Momma is gonna give me the money for it.* Whenever the orders came in and Momma inevitably didn't have the money, she would tell me, "Call your daddy and see if he will give it to you," and he always did. But that was the extent of our relationship, me calling when I needed money and him typically saying okay.

VALENTINE'S DAY

One day, Albert pulled up in front of the house in his white pickup truck and told Fallon and I to come outside. It was just before Valentine's Day. He handed us teddy bears, a box of chocolates, and Valentine's cards. It wasn't individual cards that he had spent time picking out for each of us, he hadn't written a message or signed it. It was a box of cards that you would give out to your classmates. Fallon's bear was a big honey colored bear with a red bow tied around its neck. Mine was a white teddy bear holding a bright red Hershey's kiss in between its hands. I treasured that bear because my dad gave it to me. I slept with the bear and when I wasn't cuddling it, it sat on the bookshelf above my bed.

A short while later, my middle school was hosting a father-daughter dance and Albert said he would take me. I was looking forward to having this experience with my dad for days. The night of the dance, I was all excited about going to the dance and he didn't show up. I believe he called my mom and told her he couldn't make it. In a fit of anger, I threw my white teddy bear—with the now somewhat faded red Hershey's kiss—in the trash can. I was hurt and disappointed and I didn't want anything from him. Throwing out my bear is probably one of the biggest regrets of my life. To this day, I don't know if he picked it out himself or if Jackie bought it and told him to take it to us. At the time it didn't matter, I just assumed he did it and I loved it, but because of my emotions I no longer have it.

THE VOLUNTEER

Whenever I struggled with my schoolwork, Momma always volunteered to help. I hated when I was in elementary school, and we would be working on our portfolios for the year and the teacher would say write a personal narrative or write an essay. I wanted to write what I wanted to write. Momma helped get those done. But the real frustration came in high school. I had my share of tear-filled meltdowns at the kitchen table, especially when I was trying to learn French. There were a few areas where she didn't offer to assist. When I needed help with math or science homework, she volunteered my dad. In one of my classes, we had a project to make a model rocket and I had no clue where to start. It didn't have to fly or anything; it just had to look like a rocket. Momma said, "Go to your dad's, I'm sure he'll help you figure it out." We, well he used the brown inner rolls that toilet paper and paper towel come on and he cut them and hot glued them together and that was my rocket. I got to see him in action; being creative, very quick, intelligent, and the capable man that Momma described when she talked about the reasons she was attracted to him.

By the time I was in high school, he was no longer dating Jackie and had started living with a lady named Elaine. She was the only lady he had lived with that I knew of besides Jackie. Jackie and I got along great. I babysat for her in her home, sometimes I would stay late and eat dinner with them. She loved iced coffees from Baskin Robins and would bring me back one when she got off work. After I started high school, I was no longer babysitting, so I didn't see Jackie or my brothers very much. Albert told me that I could call him at Elaine's if I needed to and I did a few times. It was an awkward situation because my mom and Elaine didn't like each other, a fact that Momma made clear. I never met her or had any interactions with her. I didn't go visit my dad at her house like I did with Jackie and my little brothers. Aside from calling the house to speak to my dad, I never had a single conversation with her. I would call and say, "Can I speak to my dad, or can I speak to Albert?", and she would call him to the phone or tell me if he wasn't home. One day I guess she got sick of my bad phone manners and told me, "You are calling my house; you should say hello to me first," or something along those lines. Teenage me didn't like that comment at all and I proceeded to tell my Momma who proceeded to cuss her out. I never called her house again. Which mind you, she was right.` I should have had better phone manners, but how she said it was rude. It would have been better for her to speak to my dad about it instead of coming to me.

9. South 4th Street Morrison Hall – Age 18 - 20

FRESHMAN ORIENTATION

Freshman Orientation weekend was our chance to pre-view life in college. Momma had to work and even if she didn't, she has never driven on the highway. I don't think we ever discussed her coming. She was still unhappy with the idea of me going away for college because #1, "You're a girl; girls don't leave," and #2, I was the baby of the family; it never crossed her mind that I would want to be anywhere but there. Moria volunteered to drive me the two hours up the highway to Louisville. When I saw the blue numbers on the front of the building and the con-crete steps leading up to the glass doors, I was both excited and anxious. I graduated from high school a few months before my 18th birthday, and the farthest I had been away from home was spending one week in Houston, TX with my brother Donald. Yes, I know that two hours isn't extremely far but for me it was. I didn't even want to stay overnight, but they explained that spending the night was part of the experience and all the other freshmen were going to be staying. I signed in at the front desk and was greeted by two peer counselors, who explained what was in store for the weekend. Moria drove back to Bowling Green, leaving me on my own. It was a fast-paced experience. After signing in, they assigned a small group of us to a peer counselor, mine was Rada. Rada promptly told us that she had ADD, while chatting animatedly about 100 other things. She gave us a tour of the campus, told us more about peer counselors, and briefed us on what to expect from campus life. She asked us a question then started talking about something else before we even had a chance to respond.

We returned to the dorms to spend the night. Correction, my Spalding friends would remind me that we don't use the term dorms anymore. It's a residence hall which is much fancier. I was not excited about the idea of having to sleep on a green plastic twin mattress that looked older than I was. The room we were given was the first room next to the stairs. I walked across the hall and found another room with an old couch and TV mounted to the wall. There was a sub-room that I believe had a toilet and tub littered with trash, beer bottles, and caps. I was horrified that this was what we were going to be using once we moved in a few weeks later. I was nearly in tears at the thought of living and sleeping in this place for the next 4 years. Thankfully, I learned that room was more of a neglected, unused lounge that each floor had, and we weren't going to be using the decrepit bathroom. I was not much happier to learn that we would be using shared showers and restrooms with everyone else on the floor. The bedrooms themselves weren't terrible but they were small, had built-in shelves above the bed, and built-in dressers. The saving grace was a good size closet. I hadn't really thought about having to sleep in a room with a stranger a few feet away. The roommate I was assigned to for orientation was this tiny feisty Belizean chick named Laurita, but everyone called her Lau. She wasn't the person I was initially going to be living with for freshman year, but we got along so well during the orientation weekend, we asked if we could keep it that way once the school year began. Usually, time away from my home and family meant spending the weekend at my girlfriend Valentina's house and that was maybe 15 minutes away. There I was intent on living 2.5 hours away, full time for the next four years and suddenly I thought, "This is the worst idea I have ever had." I was sad the first night and even called home in tears, but by Sunday morning, I had connected with some fun and welcoming people who made me excited about what Spalding University (SU) had to offer. During that first year, any time I was feeling homesick or doubting my decision, I reminded myself of what Mark had said and I would tell myself I have to stay just one more month, another session, another semester, and the longer I stayed, the more I was proving him wrong.

Katrina Carpenter, Senior Year

A few weeks later, Moria and I loaded up her silver and green Expedition with all my stuff and hit the road again. Momma didn't make the move-in day trip either, it was just me, Moria, and her husband; KJ. There were some kids like Andrea, the roommate I was originally assigned or Laurita, the roommate I chose, there with their family members. It was a building bubbling with energy, movement, and noise. Laurita's mom and brothers were there helping her get moved in. On her side of the room, she had a setup pulled straight from Pinterest. She had a perfectly fluffy, grownup white and black comforter, and a pile of pillows. She had a small black cushioned saucer chair and a freaking throw rug. Her dresser and closet were full of clothes and shoes organized neatly along with her shower shoes and caddy. She tacked up a calendar on the wall beside her dresser where she would methodically track what she wore each day for two weeks at a time so she could avoid repeating an outfit too soon. That tracking thing didn't last long, maybe a few months, but it made an impression. She was equally prepared with food and snacks, a microwave, mini fridge, and TV. Basically, she had all the things, things I didn't even think of and things not on the move in list, like this little towel-robe combo with spaghetti strap sleeves. My roomie was extra ready and just plain extra.

*Laurita and Katrina, Freshman
Year, Spalding University*

Then there were kids like me, who were dropped off and setting up their rooms on their own. I didn't really know what to expect. I didn't even think of asking anyone to stay with me or to take me on a grocery run. I just showed up with what I had. I had used money from working at the grocery store and some graduation money to get as many of the things on the new student list as I could afford. My dark blue bedding with gold stars and moons was nice, but a bit too warm and didn't feel very girly or mature compared to my roommate's. I had a micro fridge that slid nicely under the desk and a TV that weighed a ton with a built-in DVD and VHS player combo that I sat on top of my built-in chest of drawers completely blocking my view of the mirror.

Katrina Carpenter, Dorm Room

There was no cable in our rooms, if we wanted to watch anything other than our own DVDs and VHS tapes, we had to go to the basement and hope nobody else was using the television down there. We would exchange movies with other folks in the dorm once we had watched everything in our collection. Some of the students who had been living there for a while had managed to steal cable by splitting the wires through the ceiling to the only cable source in the building. Eventually my roommate and I did the same thing but it didn't last long. We had "random" room inspections, and if the Resident Advisors(RAs) happened to see a wire running from your TV through the ceiling you would be caught and forced to disconnect it. Sometimes our friendlier RAs would give us a heads up but not always. It wasn't worth the hassle having to disconnect it and then find someone to reconnect it for you a few days later. My first move was to immediately start cleaning the furniture with Pledge and Windexing the mirrors, a habit that all my dorm friends found hilarious. Nobody else cleaned with as much detail as I did. That first day was an eye opener as I observed everyone around me. My experience was a drop-off tuck and roll. We unloaded all of my belongings, and then my sister and her husband left me to organize my things on my own. Other families operated differently than mine. They showed support by physically being there and getting involved as their children left the nest. Laurita was several years older than me and had been to college back in Belize, but when she decided to come to the US for school, her family did everything they could to support her and make life there comfortable. The same was true for many of the other students there, many had financial support and emotional support as well. Even after move-in day, parents were coming to campus for visits periodically, whether it was to take their kids grocery shopping or out to eat and catch up.

My oldest brother Donald went out of state for college 20 plus years earlier. It had been too far away for Momma or anyone else to regularly go and visit. Our family didn't have a lot of experience with sending someone off to college. My sister Fallon stayed in town and went to college at Western, which was a much easier adjustment. Even though she moved on campus, she was still close to home. While my family couldn't provide a lot of financial support, and I only had one or two visits, everyone was encouraging and emotionally supportive of my decision (although Momma was a little reluctant) to go away for school. It seemed like every weekend Momma would be calling at the crack of dawn, interrupting my good sleeping-in time, to see how I was doing and how everything was going. My sister Fallon and cousin Shavon even came up to see me that first year, right around the time of our big formal dance. They helped me pick out a dress and get ready for *Moonlight in the Mansion*. When I needed extra funds for school supplies—like a camera for photography class—my brother's Donald and Derrick sent me the money. I think because our family didn't have a lot of experience with kids going off to school, we didn't really know how the process should or could work. It wasn't feasible for Momma or anyone else to regularly visit him. Fallon and Mark both stayed in Bowling Green for college, so me going to school in Louisville was new territory. I wish someone else in the family had done it before or that we had more of an idea of what other people were going to do with their kids. I didn't feel neglected or left out, but it would have been nice to have more visits and interaction with my family while I was at Spalding.

YOU'VE GOT MAIL

When I came into the front door of the dorm, I saw a white piece of paper with my name on it, pinned to the brown bulletin board. The bulletin board was covered with flyers and notes and had numerous holes from previous notes. Seeing your name on the board meant you had a package too big to fit into the tiny bank of wooden mailboxes. So, I asked Mrs. Anne, the grandmotherly lady who managed the front desk, if something had come for me. She heaved herself up from her seat and went into the little mailroom closet and handed me a box from Bowling Green with my Momma's handwriting swirled across it. Once I got upstairs and tore open the package, I found bottles of

Avon. She had sent me all kinds of smell goods. It was the sweetest thing because she was none too pleased with me going off to Louisville, and this was what she had chosen to contribute to me while I was away.

While I was getting new fragrances in the mail, my roommate was getting packages of her own. My major was Communication with a minor in Business. I had the occasional presentation and of course numerous speeches. I don't remember my professors asking us for anything specific in how we dressed aside from nothing revealing, no open-toed shoes, and no distracting jewelry. This was mostly geared towards our class on interview techniques. Her major, on the other hand, was Business, and she had presentations on a regular basis. According to her, there was an expectation that students would dress profession-ally for these presentations and Laurita took that expecta-tion seriously. Her Momma sent her brand-new clothing in the mail, several different dress suits, as well as tops and shoes to choose from.

Spalding exposed me to a variety of people and cul-tures, especially living in the dorm. There were students from Cypress, like Christina Papageorgiou, who used to sing Twinkle Twinkle Little Star at the top of her lungs every Sunday morning on her way to church. There was my girl Colette, who was shy and quiet at first and so petite that we were all shocked to learn she was a student. I remember thinking, *Ohhhh, she must be one of the student's daughters and they are allowing her to live on campus with her mom.* There was Liz from Belize, who was not the domestic type and would drag her dirty clothes to the laundromat and pay someone to wash them for her. There were a host of folks from Africa, who called each other Charlie and were always laughing and smiling. Then there was the Belizean crew, who loved music and dancing and going to Café

Kilimanjaro. Most of us were in the city alone and we didn't have parents looking over our shoulders to make sure we were getting the work done, but those close to me seemed to be pretty intent on doing well and took their time seriously. Being on our own for some of us, meant getting part time jobs off campus or doing a work-study job and getting paid through financial aid. I had both a work-study gig in the financial aid office, as well as working at the Center for Women and Families, and I used that money to buy my clothes, groceries, and pay my cell phone bill. Almost everyone had some type of way of making money, heck even if it was just working at the front desk of the dorm; I did that too. Most of us didn't have cars, so we walked everywhere, took TARC, or taxis. Bowling Green doesn't have a real public transit system, they finally got CART after I went to college which has limited operation around the projects and to a few other places. Being on a city bus was a new experience for me. I remember going to the mall with one of the girls from the dorm and she got so confused that we ended up coming back to campus late and missing our classes. That was the first and only time I missed a class. The rest of the time we would have one of the Resident Advisors (RA's) take us grocery shopping to Wal-Mart in the dorm vans or the occasional late night Taco Bell run. My friend Raven, who was roommates with Colette, ended up getting an old school BMW from her family, and we rode around in that for a bit. Laurita had a brand-new Honda CRV, which was a lot bigger and could hold more of us car-less kids. I believe the condition for her getting the car was that she get a job to help pay for gas and insurance. She worked at Dillard's in the mall for maybe a month or two before deciding it was too much to keep up with her class work and having a part-time job. Thankfully, her parents let her keep it.

Then there was me, a girl from little ole Bowling Green, Kentucky. From the projects but not a project girl, amongst people from all over the world, some smarter than me, more focused than me like Noor who had a double major and double minor, *who does that*? Some from higher social levels than mine and more traditional family backgrounds. I was there thriving and just as capable as any of them *in spite of* coming from more strained circumstances.

OCD & SUPERSTITIONS

I probably have undiagnosed mild Obsessive Compulsive Disorder (OCD). In class, I had to sit in the same seat every single time. I even asked a girl to move once because she was sitting in my spot. Dorm life does not make OCD easy. I wasn't excited about sharing the bathroom and showers with 40 other girls, but early on I determined which bathroom and shower stall I would use every single time. I woke up early on a Sunday morning and walked to the shower room. I opened the door and realized my stall was in use by my roommate Laurita. Just as I was saying, "Lau you're in my shower," a gang of birds flew out from one of the other shower stalls. I screamed "birds", slammed the door, ran into my room, and closed the door. I had never seen so many birds indoors in my entire life. It scared the hell out of me. I didn't know what to do, so I picked up my room phone and called the front desk. I quickly tried to explain to my friend Folami when he answered the phone, that there were a bunch of birds in the shower room and that my roommate was still inside. He calmly told me that he wasn't sure what to do. "I mean I can't call security, it's not like they can arrest the birds? I guess I could call maintenance, but it's Sunday and Robert doesn't work on

Sunday's." I was so mad that he was not freaking out as much as I was. He did end up calling maintenance and Robert came to the rescue. He made it noticeably clear that he was not excited about being pulled out of his house on Sunday afternoon when U of L was playing. The crazy thing is the shower room has no windows and we never figured out how the birds got inside. He was able to extract most of the birds, but a few were stuck for days in one of the adjacent bedrooms.

My mom has always talked to us about different superstitions like, *don't put your purse on the floor or you'll be broke. Don't put a hat on the bed or someone will die*, and a bird flying in the house also means someone is going to die. Well shortly after those birds broke into our shower room, I got a phone call from back home, Uncle Mitchell had passed away. It was crazy how the timing worked out.

FAMILY TIME

When I first moved to Louisville, the only family I had was my cousin Mel. She would pick me up on the weekends, so I could do laundry at her house for free. I would hang out with her and her two boys and eat home cooked food. My cousin Shavon ended up moving to Louisville while I was at Spalding and lived right down the road from the dorm. I could go visit her and drink sweet daiquiris. She was very outgoing, always inviting me to events all over the city. We would ride the city bus, TARC ,all over town. We went to a ballet performance downtown and enjoyed delicious food at *Big Hopps Restaurant,* where she worked. I had an amazing time celebrating my 21st birthday there with my family and friends.

It wasn't a long trip from BG to Louisville, but I only had one other visit to the dorm and that was Moria and KJ. They drove up one weekend and brought me groceries. Aside from that one visit, my brother Derrick was my road warrior, riding up and down the highway to come get me. Spalding operates on a sessions schedule; classes last 6 weeks and then there's a one-week break in between. The slogan was "high intensity learning" and our reward after that intense learning was a week to recover. Every 6 weeks Gonzie, as we call him, would drive up to Louisville and pick me up and drive me home to BG to spend time with my family and friends. He would catch me up on what was going on with the family, especially any drama, at least until I inevitably fell asleep in the passenger seat beside him. I somehow always managed to wake up right as we hit the Bowling Green city limit sign. And at the end of the break, he would turn around and drive me back, all while working night shift at a factory. Hell, in May of 2007, he finished working 3rd shift, downed an energy drink, and drove the 2 hours up the highway to see me graduate with honors *magna cum laude*. He was wide-eyed and tired but there for me. That's the best thing about our family: We hold each other down and everyone helps in any way that they can and we celebrate our wins.

Left to Right: Derrick Carpenter, Mark Carpenter, Donald Carpenter, Carolyn Carpenter, Katrina Carpenter in cap and gown, Fallon Carpenter, Jamal Carpenter. My college graduation in May 2006 from Spalding University

REKINDLING THINGS

The older I got, the idea of my parents getting back together had pretty much faded. One day, when I was minding my business in my dorm room, I got a call from my sister Fallon. She called me in that almost *gossipy girl you won't believe this* tone. "Tell me why Momma and Albert are practically living together?" After more than 18 years, they had decided to try again to have a committed relationship. Eventually, Momma called and nonchalantly told me they were kinda dating. I was mad. I remember thinking, *I don't need you to be in love now, I don't need you to live together or be a couple now. I'm a grown up!* It felt very selfish for them to wait until we were all adults to reconcile. The benefit of them being together had pretty much ended. My siblings were shocked and upset about it as well, especially my oldest brothers. Donald and Derrick witnessed firsthand the abuse Momma had experienced for years dealing with Albert. One incident occurred during Donald's first year in college down in Florida. One night, Momma came home from playing poker, and when she got out of the taxi Albert jumped out and was trying to fight her. The backdoor opened and Donald came out wearing some shorts and told Albert, "I'm a grown man now and I respect you as my stepfather, but you will never again put your hands on my Momma. Never again." Albert apologized and said he wasn't going to hit her and then he left. Momma didn't even know that Donald was home.

On top of all the abuse, he was a deadbeat daddy, which made things harder for Momma. Albert's lack of financial support meant that Donald and Derrick had to step up to support Momma and their younger siblings. Momma had a plan. The oldest sibling would go to college and get a job, then help the sibling under them and the next one would help the next sibling. Things didn't quite work out the way we pictured it, but both Donald and Derrick helped each of us as much as they could financially, emotionally, and physically. None of us were thrilled by their decision to try again in their old age, so to speak. Eventually, we all kind of accepted it and dealt with it in our own way. I tried to get to know my dad, but it was awkward and didn't really gain any traction. Their rekindled romance fizzled out and they went back to the familiar, on again off again; sometimes they like each other, sometimes they hate each other cycle that they've always done. The only difference is now my dad feels more comfortable coming around to visit or spend time with us on holidays, if he and my Momma are on speaking terms at the time. He comes for birthday parties and all that good stuff. He loves jumping in pictures with all his kids.

Left to Right: Mark Carpenter, Jamal Carpenter, Derrick Carpenter, Katrina Carpenter, Albert Hayes, Carolyn Carpenter, Albert Hayes Jr., Fallon Carpenter, Moria Carpenter
Momma's 70th Birthday in 2020

Momma says he is always telling people around town about his kids and what we have accomplished with so much pride. It makes her mad that he feels like he has a right to mention us and our accomplishments at all, since he had little to do with what we have achieved. Personally, I don't let it bother me. If he wants to speak highly or proudly of me or my siblings, it doesn't do me any harm. On the other hand, it is one of those things where you think, *the audacity*. Everything we have done, achieved, experienced is because of the blessings of Allah, our own efforts, and the efforts of our Momma. He has no stake in who we are or where we are. Why he feels comfortable discussing us I don't know, I haven't asked him. We excelled and achieved some amazing things, ***in Spite Of. In spite of*** growing up in poverty, *in spite of* growing up in a fatherless home, *in spite of* dealing with drug and gambling addictions in the family; I am who I am, and we are who we are, *in spite of* circumstances that have broken many. These kinds of circumstances cause some people to struggle with depression, have addiction issues of their own, turn to crime, or even become stuck. Some people look at where they are or how they grow up and decide that's all that ever will be for them. I'm an observer. I chose to look at things that were going on in my life and say, "I don't like this. This is not how I want to live the rest of my life; I want more for myself and my future." And I went out and pushed for it. Not that it is or was easy, but I decided to try for a different kind of life than I had growing up.

DADDY'S GIRL

When I go home to Bowling Green, I always stay with my mom 'cause I'm a Momma's girl. Albert has offered a few times for me to come and stay with him. Momma flipped her lid as soon as she heard him make the offer. She would have a conniption if I ever chose to spend the night at my dad's house instead of hers. For her, it's not just me staying with him, it is me choosing him over her, so that's never happened. Plus, it's a little awkward. We don't really know each other that well nor have we had a lot of deep conversations, despite both of us trying. How do you try to learn someone after decades of not having to know much about them? I find myself asking random questions about his favorite foods and desserts, especially around the holidays. On Thanksgiving, about two years ago, we made a bunch of new desserts, and I asked my dad, "What's your favorite dessert?" He said Millionaire's cake which I had never heard of or tried before. I wanted to make it for him, but we didn't have all the ingredients. It just reinforced how little I know about him. I can tell you my Momma loves steak and caramel cake, which she makes from scratch. I've never cooked for my dad, but I've cooked for the rest of the family; I haven't had the chance to impress him. There's still a little lingering desire to make my daddy happy, to make him excited about something I did, maybe just to please him.

I never properly dealt with my dad's lack of involvement in my life. It's not something that ever made me outwardly emotional when I was younger. I felt like something was missing. I just didn't express it. As much as I feel like I have been able to ignore my father's absence in my childhood, the older I get the more I realize I've got daddy issues.

Daddy's Girl

I think I coulda been a daddy's girl
I mean if he had been around

What's the saying?
Momma's boy and...
Daddy's girl

Yeah I think I coulda been a daddy's girl
I mean if he had been around

It's cool tho
I get to be my Momma's baby
My Momma's favorite
Don't worry everybody knows

I think I could have been a daddy's girl
I mean if he had been around
But I guess now I'll never know

10. South Preston Street—Age 22-29

When I was 22, I was living in my second bachelorette pad in Old Louisville. Old Louisville is filled with big, beautiful, historic mansions. Owners turn these multistory, multiroom houses into several small private apartments. I was excited to have my own private entrance on the side of the house. Everything about this apartment was small. From the kitchen to the living room was probably a few inches, from the living room to the bedroom was maybe 1 or 2 feet at most, and the bathroom was connected to the bedroom. I had to walk outside and up the front steps to the main house to check my mail or use the washer and dryer in the foyer. I was there just shy of a year, and once Fall hit and I started receiving extremely high power bills, I decided that the cost of renting a tiny one-bedroom apartment and paying utilities was ridiculous. How could a small place use as much gas and electricity as a whole house with a family. What's worse is that in Louisville, there is only one company for both electricity and gas, *Louisville Gas and Electric* (LG&E.) So, if you have a high bill to pay, you really have no choice but to come up with all the money or get disconnected. In Bowling Green, there are two separate companies, so it's possible for you to maybe not pay your electric bill to BGMU but still pay your gas bill to ATMOS Energy. There were many times when we had gas and no electric, or electric and no gas. There was no monopoly like there is in Louisville. If I was going to pay such high bills, I was going to do it in a house I owned, so I decided to buy one.

I had absolutely no idea what I was doing; from figuring out how to start searching for homes, determining how much I could afford each month for a mortgage payment, calculating how much money I would need to put up to show I was serious about buying a home (earnest money), or how much I would have to set aside for a down payment. Actually, I didn't even know you needed a down payment, but my realtor Louise was amazing. I found her when I came across a listing she had online for her own home. It wasn't the right fit for me, but she promised to help me find *the one*. She connected me to different mortgage brokers to get financing, she educated me on down payment assistance programs, and drove me around town to see home after home; making sure they met my needs and my wish list. It was an exciting process.

My family had mixed emotions. They were a cross between happy and shocked. The main reason was because I was so young and buying a house all on my own. The house I chose was the cutest little 2-bedroom shotgun-style house with a faux brick fireplace in the living room, and a huge picture window reminiscent of the one we had on 12th Avenue. It had original wood flooring and zero insulation under the crawl space which meant my feet were always freezing in the winter. The ceilings were extremely high, especially in the front bedroom which I turned into my home office. I loved opening the window and listening to the rain fall while blasting music or listening to the television filtering in from the other room while I worked on my computer. I had a cushy beige futon that I pushed against the wall and once it was pulled out, I could never manage to push it back up again on my own. The closets were non-existent, but I made it work by buying a large armoire that sat in my office and held blankets, sheets, and curtains.

I had been living there for a year or two, when my friend, Beth Ann, from Spalding asked if she could move in with me until she went off to the Peace Corp. She was bunking in the office on the futon with her dog Juneau, who was the funniest little runt of a dog I've ever met. She would quietly stalk you when you ate and was even known for sneaking food and creeping out of the room to eat stolen goods.

SNOW AND ICE

In January of 2009, there was a terrible ice storm that devastated several states including Kentucky. I was getting my Masters of Communications degree at the University of Louisville and working my first real job at Humana Insurance company. Louisville was hit hard; 205,000 people lost power and it took up to 10 days to get everyone hooked back up. Several emergency shelters were set up across the affected region. The storm caused the largest power outage on record for the state of Kentucky, impacting more than half a million people at its height and for more than a 100,000 of those impacted; the outages lasted more than a week. Falling trees and large limbs weighed down by the ice caused widespread property damage. My house was spared any damage, but we did lose power. The ice storm also brought death, killing 65 people nationwide and 35 in Kentucky. (January 2009 North American ice storm, 2020) The deaths included several of the brave linemen who had traveled to Kentucky from other states to help restore power to the city as quickly as possible. Most deaths, however, were attributed to carbon monoxide poisoning due to power generators or kerosene heaters being used indoors without proper ventilation. It was sobering to hear about all the death and destruction and to think that as a child our family had relied on the warmth of a kerosene heater and were so fortunate to not suffer any mishaps while doing so.

Beth grew up poor too and had her own life hacks. Our upbringing gave us some combined survival skills, so the storm, while unfortunate and dangerous, ended up being only a moderate inconvenience and didn't impact us as much as it could have. We did what we could in the daylight. If we needed electricity for things like schoolwork, we would go to the coffee shop or somewhere else and use their power and internet. We also limited what food we purchased to things we could keep in a cooler. Beth taught me that it's possible to cook on top of the stove even when your electricity is off if you have a gas stove. Beth still had to go to work, so she would head downtown early. That part of the city was operating as usual because all the power lines there were buried underground. She would wash her hair in the sink and then dry it with paper towels and an extra Starbucks apron alongside the homeless folks who were bathing in the restroom, before heading in for her shift as a barista at Starbucks. To keep her room warm, she would heat a rock on the stove and then carry it on a plate to her room and place it beside the futon so it would be warmer at night while she slept. She even exercised by doing jumping jacks to have a little warm cocoon to sleep in. Beth was one of the first to volunteer after Hurricane Katrina. She was down in New Orleans helping to rebuild. So, when she wasn't home, she was at her church helping with the shelter that had been established for the elderly members of the community who were at high risk of death if they stayed in their homes without food or power.

GOING TO THE CHAPEL

I have always loved the song, "Going to the Chapel," by the Dixie Cups. I imagined that song playing in the background on my wedding day as I got dressed, had my makeup done, and drove to my own chapel of love. In reality, my wedding day was much more hectic. I don't remember listening to any music as I got dressed, and my cousin tied the strings of my corset style dress. Heck, I wasn't even sure my fiance and his family would make it to the venue on time. My brother Donald and I decorated the venue beautifully with purple and cream flower petals, lanterns, and floating candles in clear glass vases. Technically, it wasn't a chapel, a church, or even a mosque; it was a cottage.

In November of 2014, just one day after Thanksgiving, I married Muhammad, at Cornerstone Cottage after endless phone calls and traveling back and forth from Kentucky to Georgia for over a year. Two weeks later, he drove from Houston, Texas to Louisville in a black pickup truck and trailer to help me pack up my house and make the move to the apartment we had picked out together by video chat. I hate moving and kept thinking I had plenty of time to get it all done and delayed longer than I should have. I was overwhelmed with all the things I had to find a box for and all the things I still had to get rid of either by selling or donating. My cousin Mel was there as usual, helping me get packed and organized when my husband arrived and took charge. He was so patient with my lack of progress and didn't complain at all as he got to work breaking down furniture and loading up the truck. We slept on the bedroom floor that last night in my first home.

The next morning, as I said goodbye to the house I had spent the last 7 years in and locked the door for the very last time, I broke down crying. I felt like a real grownup in my house, an independent woman who had done something many people didn't understand. I bought a home all on my own. I was proud of myself and the fact that I had done it and didn't need anyone to help me. I managed the mortgage and the bills by myself and never had my lights or gas turned off. The only service that ever got turned off was my water bill. The previous owner had the bill going to a P.O. box and not the house. I didn't know there was a bill or that it needed to be in my name. I never had a water bill in my apartment but once I found out, I had it switched to my name and mailed to the house.

I experienced so much in that house, like my first backyard cookout with my Spalding friends Raven and NayNay. We bought this cheap grill from Dollar General that we put together haphazardly. Raven used so much lighter fluid that it nearly set the only tree in my yard on fire. The branches were long and the leaves hung down low. When that first whoosh of fire went up, we had to back up. I constantly hosted events like Ramadan iftar dinners, game nights, movie nights, pajama parties, and sleepovers with my bestie Amanda Brown. When we weren't at the house, Amanda and I did our single ladies thing, hanging out at our married friends' homes, going to dinner constantly, drinking coffee at local shops, and just enjoying late nights all over town. I made great sister friends living in that house and connected deeply to my religion. I also experienced so much loneliness and longing in that house and with good and bad it was all coming to an end. I was preparing to start a new chapter of my life that was equally exciting and scary. When my husband asked me why I was crying, I told him "I'm just realizing I will never live here again." We climbed into the truck and drove off as the snow began to fall.

11. Dairy Ashford Road - Age 29

I moved to Houston for love and for the promise of good weather. When I left Louisville, in December of 2014, it was snowing, and I was wearing a hoodie and tennis shoes. When we arrived at our apartment on Dairy Ashford Road, it was a good 80 degrees, and the landscapers were cutting the grass. That wasn't something you would ever see in Kentucky in the winter, but we weren't in Kentucky anymore. Most days you'll catch Texans in cowboy boots, flip flops, and summer wear unless it's the rainy season then you might catch them in rain boots. My husband used to say Houston only has two seasons: summer and rainy season. The rainy season can be crazy with tropical storms and hurricanes. Yes that's right, hurricanes in the desert. I don't care what anyone says, Houston is the desert. The thunderstorms were so intense that car alarms and security alarms would constantly be set off. I had never been through anything like the storms we get here.

The best thing about working for "Humana" was being able to keep my job and work remotely from my apartment. It took about a week or so before I received my equipment, but as soon as it came, I was back to some sense of normalcy. Our place was beautiful and in a gated apartment complex with a nice pool and gym. I could walk out my front door and down to the Kroger at one end of the road and two other grocery stores at the other end. It was an area for middle class young people and young families. My husband was working as a contractor for HP Computers. I was put in charge of getting the house in order and unpacking everything, which I did slowly but surely. As we neared the last few months of our lease, we started talking about whether we should renew our lease or if we wanted to consider buying a home. Now, this wasn't my first home buying rodeo and I knew it was going to be a lot of work but it was also an exciting process. We decided to give our notice and began looking at houses for sale in our neighborhood. Our rent was about $1100 or $1200 ,so we figured we could afford something similar for a mortgage. The home prices in the Energy Corridor where we lived were well above what we were expecting. I'm talking $300,000 or more. I bought my first house for $95,000. We couldn't afford anything in our area and started looking further out.

We were basically in the middle of the city of Houston. Talking with a realtor and doing online searches, we discovered houses in the Northern part of the city were much more affordable. We drove out and looked at different new home developments. We found a home that I fell in love with listed at below market price. We went through the loan process and got approved. After another few months of back and forth with the financing company, on a Thursday afternoon, we were finally able to have our signing day and get our keys to our first home together. Friday morning, my husband went off to work at Hewlett Packard. When he came home that evening, he gave me some shocking news. Hewlett Packard had ended his contract and he no longer had a job. In less than 24 hours, we went from on top of the world to being knocked off our feet and it was too late to back out.

12. Archer Glen Drive - Age 30 - present

ROUGH START

Buying a new home can be stressful. Buying a new home and then having your household income cut in half is a different level of stress. It was our 2nd year of marriage and the thought of furnishing a home, paying a mortgage, and all the bills that came with it was a lot. My emotions were all over the place. I was excited to buy all the things we needed, to paint the house and decorate, but I was also worried that we couldn't afford to do it all while living on a single income. Neither of us had a lot of money in savings and we were living paycheck to paycheck or direct deposit to direct deposit. When we bought our home, I suggested that we get something we could afford off just one of our salaries as a precaution. I didn't think that we would be doing just that immediately. I decided not to sell my house back home in Kentucky and chose to rent it out instead. So on top of being able to pay the mortgage in Texas, I still had to make sure I had enough money in my account to cover the mortgage there in case my tenants didn't pay on time, which happened way too often.

It was a lot to manage and led to tension in the marriage. I was constantly anxious that we wouldn't be able to afford it all and that it was too much pressure on me. We met with a counselor who suggested we create a budget and have regular meetings to discuss our finances. That helped to a certain extent, but it was still frustrating for me to be the main earner. I was filled with regret about agreeing to buy a house and not continuing to rent. Honestly our rent and our mortgage were about the same amount each month and owning made more sense, but all my negative thoughts and childhood struggles were freaking me out. My husband was much more optimistic and less frazzled by this setback. He started to drive for Uber and worked part time as a Domino's Pizza delivery driver, doing whatever he could to bring in money. We never missed a mortgage payment; no utilities were turned off and we didn't go hungry. It took several months, but he was able to get a new job making even more money than the job he lost.

Over the next couple of years, my husband changed jobs multiple times, going from one contract role to another. Some of the companies like *Draka Marine Oil and Gas* shutdown an entire department, *Gurwitch Products LLC* relocated to another state, giving the employees the option to move with them or be let go. While he changed companies more times than I could keep up with, I always had the stability of *Humana*.

Service and Security
ID 72034026 © Thomaskelley | Dreamstime.com

Eleven years, eleven months, and ten days of service and dedication.

Years of service were something we celebrated as an organization at milestone years, 1, 3, 5, 10 and so on and so on. These years were celebrated with certificates, luncheons down at the corporate building, and the right to choose from a variety of gifts that got better and better the longer you had been with the company. Eleven years, eleven months, and ten days of relative stability. Eleven years, eleven months, and ten days of security. Eleven years, eleven months, and ten days of answering to one supervisor and then another and then another because one thing we learned at my job was the only constant is change. Well, the last few months weren't so secure, and change was definitely coming.

I wanted to work for *Humana* for a while based on the experience of my college friend Marcie. She was hired right after she graduated and seemed to really enjoy working there. *Humana* is one of the largest employers in the city of Louisville and has been named a Fortune 500 company year after year. There is a certain level of prestige or respect for folks who work there. There are even jokes about it in the black community. *Guys just want a girl who works at Humana and they have a job at Ford.* I had applied multiple times for a variety of positions, and all I got for my efforts was those auto-generated rejection emails after rejection emails. No explanation as to why I wasn't good enough for even a phone interview. I had given up on ever working there and was focusing on getting into graduate school at the University of Kentucky in Lexington, so it didn't really matter if I got a new job in Louisville since I wasn't going to be there much longer anyway. I was able to pay my bills just fine for my tiny studio-ish apartment in a sub-divided mansion in Old Louisville. I found the apartment on Craig's List and was in love with the cozy space which was basically an attic level apartment where the walls and ceiling met at a slant and were so low, I could touch them without standing on my tip toes. The bedroom and living room were separated by a real door, but they were so small they should have just been one room. I bought a TV stand and other little items and paid my boyfriend Johnathan in spaghetti to build them. The kitchen was barely big enough for a dining table, but I had one anyway. The real jewel of the entire place was the kitchen window that you could open by turning the handle and pushing out. I could climb out and sit on the roof, something I did maybe once, and admire the beautiful gardens and architecture of the surrounding homes. The furniture delivery guys were not happy with the lack of elevator and couldn't even fit my sofa up the narrow staircase and ended up having to swap it out for two loveseats instead. The 'no elevator' became an issue for me too once I sprained my ankle and was on crutches. But it was the perfect first apartment.

I had a job working at the Center for Women and Families. It was laid back and convenient. I usually worked second shift 4:00 p.m.-12:30 a.m., but I preferred to dip out at midnight when my relief came on duty. Tina was more of a stickler for the rules, and I don't think she liked me skipping lunch and leaving once she showed up, but she was much older than me and we had nothing in common, so I never felt like hanging around to chat with her. Plus, I was walking home in the dark in downtown Louisville, which in hindsight was stupid crazy. Praise God, I was never bothered by anybody and made it home safely night after night. The Center as we called it, is a domestic violence and rape crisis center and shelter. My girlfriend Ayana had been working there as a PRN Crisis Counselor while going to school at Spalding and helped me get hired my senior year on a PRN basis as well. I loved being able to walk out of the front door, cross the campus parking lot and the grocery store parking lot, and be at work in less than 5 minutes. There was only one other building in between the shelter and that was Kroger, which was a blessing to broke, car-less college students which I and most of my friends were. It was also a safe travel distance for the women in the shelter who didn't want to venture too far from the sanctuary of those double security doors, iron gate, and security cameras. Once I graduated, I was offered a full-time position which was awesome and thankfully, it was not far from my new place. I could still walk to and from work.

Working at The Center was both rewarding and challenging. Most days, I felt like I was making a difference answering calls from women in distress, seeking a listening ear, or help coming up with a safety plan to escape their abuser. It was all worth it. There were also days when the calls came from sickos pretending to be sexual assault victims only interested in going into detail about their sexual experience. There was at least one guy who got a kick out of calling our crisis line and every staff member was warned about him. Other days it was like managing a zoo, shelter residents could be lazy and not interested in working, doing their chores, or watching their small children. Some took advantage of the services and the shelter, willing to manipulate staff and each other. The work was humbling but not my passion. I couldn't see myself doing it long term, but it was paying the bills while I prepared for grad school and my future career as a Public Relations Professional. I had a plan, and this was just a step in the journey, so it didn't matter if I wasn't absolutely thrilled with my work.

I was in the middle of my shift, when I got the call for an interview with *Humana*. I was so shocked that I told the recruiter, "Are you sure you meant to call me, because you guys usually immediately reject all my applications?" The recruiter explained a little bit about the position and scheduled an in-person interview for a few days later. I went to the interview dressed for success, no open-toed shoes, no dangly or distracting jewelry, and going over all the public speaking and interview tips I had ever learned in my head. Don't use conversational fillers "like or um." And remember in the words of one of my favorite Communication Professors,

Dr. Deborah McGee, "You're not nervous, you're excited." I don't remember a single question they asked me, but it went great. I left the interview with a job offer.

My first role with *Humana* was as an Enrollment Specialist processing pending applications. I didn't remember applying for that specific position, but I had applied for so many, and it was a way to get my foot in the door. During the first week of training, the instructor Patty, from the National Education and Policy Department (NEPD), was packing on the information. I was learning so much and excited to have my first corporate job. I had to be at the office by 8 a.m. for training down on the first floor. I picked up the information quickly and was always willing to answer questions and help other people in my training class who were struggling to grasp the material. After about 6 weeks, we were released to the floor to start doing the work we had been trained to do. It was a little bit overwhelming, initially, to be handling applications for real people, not dummy info in a training environment. We were surrounded by the other teams of people who had been in the department for a while. Not being in the safety of the training rooms was intimidating, but we also had access to Subject Matter Experts (SMEs) who we could call on when we got stuck. The SMEs were knowledgeable and patient with all of us and I admired them for being the go-to people in the department.

Working as an Enrollment Specialist, I learned a lot about processes and procedures. There was documentation explaining practically every single step of the work. Those documents didn't always make sense and sometimes your scenario wasn't addressed by the documentation, so when you couldn't figure out what to do, you could ask for help from a Subject Matter Expert (SME) or a team lead. These were associates who had been doing the work for a long time and had become masters at figuring things out and helping other associates learn and get up to speed. When they didn't have an answer, they knew who to turn to for even more guidance. I'm a fast learner but even I needed the occasional assistance of the SMEs and team leads. After a while, I realized that there were easier ways to do some of the things we were asked to do and began sharing this with my teammates and the supervisors. I decided I wanted to be a helper, an SME, showing people the ropes and helping influence the process. That first year, I was constantly writing up suggestions and ideas for process changes and sending them to my manager, who would then send them on to our Process Team. I was so good at analyzing issues and suggesting process changes that I was asked to be a part of a group of people who helped review process documents in our internal database called Mentor. We received a list of documents to review for accuracy on a periodic basis and then submitted any feedback for inaccuracies. I was also able to submit Mentor feedback directly to the National Education and Process Department (NEPD) without having to go through a supervisor or team lead first; my knowledge was taken as sufficient. However, I didn't see much response to my process change suggestions. I learned that it was a completely different team that handled creating and changing processes and those people were known as Process Analysts and Process Consultants.

THE INTERN

After about 3 years, I moved from being an Enrollment Specialist processing pending applications to being an Special Operations Specialist. I had applied to be on the Special OPS team the year before and had an absolutely awful interview. It was the middle of the winter, and I had just been diagnosed with bronchitis. I couldn't think or breathe, all I wanted to do was to rest. I wasn't surprised when I received the rejection email. Then a year later when my supervisor told me that I was being placed on the Special Operations team, I wasn't excited. I kept thinking, *I already interviewed and the supervisor didn't want me then, now he is being forced to take me.* Our team was the last stop for resolving member issues, from enrollment delays, rejected enrollments, agent errors to privacy issues, and grievance and appeals complaints. Once I joined the team, I excelled and had an awesome relationship with my supervisor Byron. Many people were intimidated by him and avoided expressing themselves to him. I was never intimidated and always told him exactly what was on my mind. He was really nice and caring, but his physical appearance as a big, tall, former football player scared some folks. I was the go to person for training new associates and for interacting with other departments. Associates in other areas would reach out to me specifically for assistance and really enjoyed working with me and respected the effort I would go to for our members.

My supervisor, Byron, told me that the Process team had created an internship program that would give me the chance to learn the ins and outs of what went into creating the processes we used daily. It gave me an opportunity to sit in on meetings and finally make the changes that were needed. I was excited to be even closer to my goal of influencing processes and was eager to work with the Process Consultant I had been assigned to. Her name was Kelley and she had no actual experience in the department she supported and had come over to the Process department from working in a corporate office position. She already had an intern, Jennifer, who I knew. I had been one of the

SMEs in her training class. Kelley essentially handed me off to Jennifer and had her instructing me on what to do and when. It was far from what I thought it was going to be and was quite embarrassing to have someone with less time, knowledge, and experience than me oversee me. I would do all the work that Kelley asked me to do and then email it to her only to have her ask me what I had done and basically waste my time. I decided that while the idea of interning seemed great, the actual experience was not helping me and ended my internship early.

THE PROCESS TEAM

It took me about 8 years to get a role I had been wanting as a Process Analyst. I kept hearing that you couldn't just join the Process Team, you have to work your way up to it by taking on other roles first, like being a Team Lead. I wasn't really interested in being a Team Lead, but I applied when a position opened up. I thought the interview went great until I received the rejection email explaining that they didn't think I would be a good fit because I talked too fast. The audacity of someone telling me a girl with a Masters degree in Communication, that I wasn't a good communicator was beyond me. *In spite of* that initial rejection, I stayed the course and became a Team Lead a few years later, I was finally getting close to my goal.

I had a video interview with an old colleague, Stacey, who knew my quality of work and level of productivity, as well as my ability to express process change suggestions. There was another interviewer there as well, a department manager named Jessica. I couldn't tell how I had done from their energy and expressions on the screen, but at the end of the day I was offered the position and dived right in. Within a month or so, I was told that Stacey was switching positions and would no longer be my supervisor. My new supervisor would be Andrea. Working with her was great. She was extremely helpful and patient with me learning the different systems and even let me take on extra responsibilities, like uploading documentation from regulatory agencies into internal databases. Less than a year later, Andrea received a promotion. So, I had a third supervisor, Jennifer. She was a supportive manager as well, but I soon learned that an entirely new team was being created within the process world that would focus on member experience. We were given the option to either stay in traditional process improvement, working directly with an assigned operational area, or join the new team. I was up for the challenge and the idea of being a part of creating something new. The new team would be the Process Improvement- Member Experience Team.

MEETING WITH A SPECIAL GUEST

The most constant thing about working at *Humana* is change. One day you are reporting to one supervisor and by the next day you learn that you have a new one. When I first started working from home, associates had to meet very strict criteria to qualify, including meeting production and quality metrics and having good attendance. You also had to have approval from your manager. Very few associates were participating in the program and many managers didn't allow it. The company, over the years, became more open to remote or teleworking. Most of our meeting invites came with an attached Webex link. My team had folks in four states and five cities. The only time we met in person was for quarterly department meetings or the occasional team touch base, in which case we all gathered in Louisville, Kentucky. To get a random team meeting invite from our supervisor was usually no big deal, until it was. Included on the invite was a "special guest," Carolyn from HR. Instant panic spread from Instant Messenger to Instant Messenger and offline phone calls lead to even deeper anxiety. None of us had any idea what this meeting could be about, but we weren't optimistic. Mind's racing, we tried to figure out what in the heck was going on, was our supervisor leaving, were we getting a new one, were they going to create another new team like they did when our group was formed? None of this really would require the presence of HR. All we knew was we had the rest of the day and all night to worry.

The next day during the meeting we were informed by our supervisor, Jessica, that our department was going to be downsizing and eliminating certain role types such as my role as a Process Improvement Professional 2 (aka Process Analyst) and the roles of several other members of my team. Humana went through several other large scale layoffs, including one in 2010, where 1400 jobs were eliminated. The stress at the time was high for all of us, as we anxiously waited to see if we were going to be let go. I survived the 2010 layoff and a few others that followed, and now I was once again on edge.

One of the hardest punches to the gut was learning that several people had nothing to worry about. Our team project manager was going to be reassigned to another team, the two newest hirers— whom we had helped onboard and got up to speed—were both safe as they had different role types than most of us. Essentially, out of an eight-person team, three people were safe and five of us were facing elimination. We had the option to apply for a new role on our current team, but the requirements were different than the current requirements and we were not guaranteed to make the team. Another punch was knowing we had done nothing wrong, yet we were hit with this uncertainty. The final punch was wondering if our supervisor had fought for us, if she was telling the truth about it being a department wide downsize, or if she had wanted to get rid of us.

The conversations after that initial meeting were so emotional. I worked closely with one of the consultants on my team, Rosemary. "Are you okay?" she asked. I managed to get out, "I'm in shock," while trying not to cry. "What about you?" I asked. "To be honest, I have been applying for other positions for a while now." I think that response shocked me too. Rosemary managed a project focused on implementing a new system called Verint into several operational areas that were production based. Since I was the only analyst on the team, I was assigned to assist her with that project by scheduling meetings, taking notes, and essentially learning how to be a project manager. She was an informal mentor for me. We both lived in Texas, which made it easier for us to team up. We chatted often about work and life outside the office. She is funny, feisty, and even shorter than me. We connected even more during the year when we traveled back and forth to Louisville for the team meetings. I had no idea she was trying to get a new position and didn't realize she was unhappy or dissatisfied with how the team was going. I asked her if she planned to reapply for the team or if she was only interested in something new, and she expressed that she wasn't interested in staying. I spoke with several other ladies on the team, we only had one guy among us. I talked to my friend, Candace, who was angry but optimistic that we could find new roles. She had no plans to reapply for our same team and didn't try to hide her disdain for the position we were put in. She was bolder than most of us, especially when it came to the department wide meeting to discuss plans for the upcoming year. Our boss told us that we were all still invited to come to the department's meeting in Louisville and that we could use the time to connect with other areas and network for potential positions. We weren't required to attend but we were more than welcome to do so and to use the time to our advantage or we could skip it with no hard feelings. Everyone attended but Candace who used that time to apply and interview for other positions.

We were given three months to start applying for other positions within the company. We were expected to continue performing our work, despite the dark thunder cloud hanging over us every day. Because we were facing unemployment, we were paired with a recruiter from Human Resources who would help keep us at the top of the list for any position we applied for during the last 90 days. Again, we were not promised an interview, but they would make any other recruiters or hiring managers aware that we were facing a role elimination which might garner us some greater consideration than other associates who were just applying for the role but not facing unemployment. Honestly, all the HR recruiters did was send us a weekly list of new positions that had been posted to the job board. They didn't search for potential roles for us, they didn't suggest new departments that we might be qualified for, they just checked in periodically and sent us a giant Excel spreadsheet every Monday of hundreds of jobs that we could filter and search on our own. If we couldn't find a new position within that time, we would be let go and given a severance package.

STAGES OF GRIEF

After nearly 12 years, the company I had been growing up with, was abandoning me. I was devastated to think that I was so disposable. I had been a hardworking and valuable member to every team and department I had been on and couldn't understand why they were fine with losing me. Don't get me wrong, I had applied for jobs with other companies and in other industries over the years trying to find a career that was more in line with my educational background in Communication. I emailed one HR manager multiple times with no response, until I noticed I had been spelling her name wrong; oops. She finally responded. Despite a few interviews, I didn't get any offers. Most of the companies couldn't provide a salary comparable to the one I was making at *Humana* and thus, wouldn't offer me a job. But while I was with *Humana*, I gave it my all, exceeding both quality and production standards, leading department training, and championing projects that had broad impacts, not just for our associates but our members as well. I did everything I could to be a valued member of the company. I went through the stages of grief a few times. Some days I was in total shock, other days I was angry, a few days I was perfectly content with things and had accepted that it was for the best. On at least one or a few days, I was so hurt I would burst into tears sitting in my home office. Staring at the dual monitors, the office phone, and the beautifully framed diplomas on the wall, realizing it was all coming to an end. The indignation that I was being let go, "How dare they?" was real.

90 DAY COUNTDOWN

During those 3 months, I searched for new roles that I would enjoy and could do remotely. It took me a long time to make it to the Process Team, and I was feeling the most fulfilled I had ever been since I was hired in 2007. Friends and teammates graciously sent me suggestions for other positions they thought I should apply for, and others promised to keep their eyes out. While I appreciated the help, most of the roles didn't really appeal to me. I didn't want to move into a random position, and I didn't want to be stuck doing something that would bring me a paycheck but not happiness. Because our company is based in Kentucky, and I live in Texas, it was more difficult to get a new position. While *Humana* is open to remote work, many hiring managers are not, or only allow it for associates who live in the same city as the position is based in. Unfortunately, there aren't many roles like that in Houston. I think the only office building locally is a customer service call center. I applied for a few roles, some I was genuinely interested in and some I wasn't thrilled about but was willing to consider. Some were remote based and some were not, but I hoped that the hiring manager would allow me to work remotely in time, even if I had to be onsite for training temporarily. Despite my efforts and the *special assistance* of HR, I was never offered an interview for any of those roles. I started to wonder if my current supervisor was blackballing me. Part of the internal application process requires your current manager to give a performance reference to the hiring manager of any position you apply for. Ordinarily, I would have no doubt that I would be receiving outstanding feedback from my manager, but a few months before the downsizing announcement there had been some tension between her and I.

We had a team meeting in Louisville to discuss plans for the team for the year and what direction we were going to take as far as skills we would focus on and types of projects we would tackle. My supervisor was explaining the direction she wanted us to go in, and for me it seemed like a huge change from how we had operated up to that point. We had focused on things in her words, "from the ground level, in the weeds," based on our operational knowledge and experience, and she wanted us to start "looking at things from a balcony perspective." We were all expected to obtain Six SIGMA certifications, which is a great tool to have and looks great on a resume, however, taking time to obtain the certifications had not been a priority for me. For years, *Humana* emphasized the concepts found in the book *Strength Finders,* which suggests that instead of spending all your time focusing on your weaknesses and things you may not be good at, focus on those things you are good at; your personal strengths. This idea really hit home for me because it isn't what we normally hear. If you struggle at math, you should get a tutor or practice more, if you aren't good at money management, then establish a budget and so on and so forth. But finally, someone was saying that we don't have to all be good at everything. I'm great at analyzing a situation, I'm a great communicator and can explain things easily in a way that others understand. I suck at numbers and analyzing large amounts of data, so I tend to avoid work that requires having to deal with numbers. The new plan and expectations felt overwhelming. I expressed my concern and my fears in what I thought was a respectful way and what should have been a safe environment. I was wrong. My boss responded in a way that made me feel embarrassed for expressing how I felt and unsafe being honest with her. She said that anyone that didn't like the new direction we were going in was free to find another position. I returned to Houston after that meeting feeling like I no longer wanted to be a part of that team and no longer wanted her as my manager. So that negative interaction weighed on my mind when I saw no traction with my applications or requests for interviews. The more I thought about the idea of leaving *Humana,* the more I realized that it might not be the worst thing that could happen to me.

13. Aspiring Entrepreneur

After our team meeting with HR, we had one-on-one meetings with the same representative who discussed our individual situations. During the meeting, she explained what would happen in the event we were unable to secure a new position. One of the things I learned was that on top of a severance package that would continue to pay my salary for 6 months, I would also have access to the money in my company sponsored 401K managed by Charles Schwab. I could roll that money over to a new company once I found another job or manage my own 401K. The government has a special rule that allows you to use the funds in your 401K to create a self-funded and self-managed 401K. You can use those funds to invest in starting your own business or purchasing an existing business. I had been investing in my 401K for nearly 12 years and my account was looking great. I had enough money to really consider starting my own business and not rush to find another job.

The idea of owning my own business is one that I had thought about on and off for over a decade. Years ago, I convinced my friend John to let me sell accessories, scarves, and jewelry at a community festival under his company name. It was an exciting experience, finding companies to get products from and setting up the accounts. It was a little stressful running the booth mostly alone, and I experienced some hiccups since I had no experience doing something like that. Heck, I usually was the customer on the other side of the table, happily buying goods at the festival, not thinking about the logistics of having a booth. I was so excited to get started that first day. I showed up with no cash to make change, which proved particularly challenging when my first customer showed up ready to make a purchase. Fortunately, John was still there and was able to go make change for me and in the meantime, I was able to use a Square Credit card app and card reader. It wasn't perfect, but it was my first attempt, and I was proud of myself for trying. After the festival, I struggled to sell my remaining products online to my Facebook friends but that was a bust. I didn't know how to take the business to the next level or what my next move should be, so I ended up not doing anything else with the idea. I didn't even know who to ask or where to start. I'm not sure why I didn't ask my friend, who was a successful small business owner for many years, for advice.

Leaving *Humana* would give me the opportunity to finally have a business of my own. I started thinking about what things I was passionate about and what ways I could turn those passions into money making endeavors. One of my biggest passions is playing games, all kinds of games, from board games like Monopoly or Sorry; to trivia games like Tip of the Tongue and Know it or Blow It, and interactive games like Operation, Pie Face, and HeadBandz. I love any chance to play games, whether it is a family gathering, a volunteer event, or as a team building activity at work. If friends invite me over, I'm probably going to bring a game, that's just where I get my joy. So, I started talking with friends and family about how I could get paid for my passion.

My best friend Amanda and I talked about it for days, and she mentioned that her husband used to go to a coffee shop that had board games you could play for free. She told me how he really enjoyed playing games when he would go there with friends and that maybe I should include food and drinks in my plan. Y'all this was essentially the idea I had been playing around with in my head. I wanted to offer games and of course great treats to people wanting to get out of the house and socialize either amongst themselves or with others in their community. I wanted to offer a gathering spot for my community and those like myself who enjoy playing games, but either don't want to invest in a bunch of games that they may or may not love or will play once or twice and then never again. You can't play trivia games more than a few times before you've learned all the answers. Another thing to consider is that sometimes we just prefer to get out of the house and interact with others. The Coronavirus Pandemic has shown how much we crave social interaction. So, I started doing some research, Googling things like board game cafes and found that this was an actual thing someone else had already thought of. There are no original ideas as they say. But this didn't deter me as it might have in the past when I realized an idea I had wasn't so unique. Instead, it boosted my excitement and eagerness to bring the café to life and put my unique spin on it.

Of course, Googling led to Facebook, where I came across an ad for a 5 Day Workshop called *Validate Your Business Idea* with a focus on indoor play café concepts created by Michele Caurana. Michele is a play café owner with a background in business finance and marketing, who helps would-be entrepreneurs realize their dream of play café ownership. The 5-day workshop was a springboard for brainstorming and formulating my idea and then expanding that idea into a business plan and website for my dream business, *Time to Play Café.* It also led to joining the *Play Café Academy,* an online learning program that helps guide you through starting a play café; from creating a business plan to learning different ways to obtain funding. It also gave practical insight on the day-to-day operation of a play café from purchasing café equipment and toys to creating birthday party packages. I was able to join a private Facebook group called *Play Maker Society,* filled with other entrepreneurs who are existing café owners or folks working to bring their dreams to life. The group is amazing, filled with people who are extremely collaborative, insightful, and supportive.

When I was younger, my mom and my brother Derrick had dreams of opening a juke joint (club and restaurant). They didn't have enough money to get it started on their own, so they tried to apply for SBA funding. The SBA officer told them they needed a business plan first. Neither of them had ever written a business plan, had no relevant educational background, and had no prior experience owning a business. They had no idea where to start but they tried. They turned in the business plan to the SBA and they were rejected, the business plan wasn't correct, so they tried again and got rejected again. I don't know how many times they wrote business plan after business plan only to be denied. Nobody ever sat down with them and told them exactly what they needed to include or how to get started. They didn't have any friends who could tell them what to do, and how to write a business plan isn't something you learn in high school. They were never able to get the funding they needed.

Writing a business plan in 2020 was much easier for me. First, I had helped a friend write his business plan several years earlier, mostly copy editing, but it gave me insight into the process and the types of information that was needed. I had previously helped Muhammad and his friends write their business plan for their start-up mobile mechanic business *CHNGr Automotive*. They found an online tool for creating business plans. The web-based application called *LivePlan*, contains sample business plans for a variety of business types, you can download and then plug and play your own information. Or you can completely start from scratch, and it will take you step-by-step by asking you questions, showing you examples, and then plugging in your answer to create a professional business plan. The amazing thing about *LivePlan* is that you can enter data and change it at will, and the system will automatically recalculate your changes without having to do it all manually. It also has an option to create multiple plans or versions of the same plan and make changes without having to manually do all the work from scratch repeatedly. It saves you so much time and offers a ton of information, examples, and guidance. This is something my mom and brother never had access to but could have benefited from had it been around back then.

After I completed my business plan through *LivePlan*, I contacted my local SBA to figure out the next steps in getting funding. They suggested I meet with someone from SCORE. According to the SCORE website, "SCORE, the nation's largest network of volunteer, expert business mentors, is dedicated to helping small businesses get off the ground, grow, and achieve their goals." They help validate business ideas and plans to help potential business owners secure SBA funding to finance their new businesses or help purchase existing businesses. The mentors range from retirees of major corporations, as well as former and current business owners. They also host seminars, online trainings, and on-demand courses relevant to business ownership, such as how to get funding, how to manage your bookkeeping needs, and hundreds of other things. I was able to meet with a Certified Mentor by the name of Anil Prasad. He quickly, yet strategically, scanned the business plan, gave me insight on how to organize it better, based on what things the loan officers would focus on the most, what questions they would ask, and how to address those things in my plan. He was impressed with the thoroughness and work I had put into the business plan, but he also had a lot of questions I wasn't expecting and wasn't able to answer off the top of my head. Thankfully, Muhammad had gone with me and was able to speak numbers and data in a way I couldn't but needed to be able to, to secure funds. That one meeting gave me an idea of what to expect once I was ready to meet with banks.

UNITY BANK

During the meeting with my SCORE mentor, I asked him for suggestions on which banks I should apply to for an SBA loan. Based on his experience and the size of the loan I was seeking, which was about $300,000, he suggested I apply with a smaller local bank and gave me a list of several banks I could research and consider. I read up on all of them and decided that I wanted to try *UNITY National Bank,* a black-owned community bank here in Houston. I scheduled an appointment to meet with the SBA loan manager, Linda Guidry and Mark Danford, the President and CEO of *Waterstone LSP*, which is a larger bank that helps manage and process the loan applications for *UNITY*. I wasn't expecting Mark to be there, but it did give me some good feelings knowing he has the same name as one of my brothers. Both Mark and Linda responded very well to the concept of a play café and seemed positive about the progress I had made with the business plan and my thoughts on potential locations. They emailed me a ton of paperwork to complete as part of the application process. I had to explain who would be running the business, list all my assets and liabilities, provide a detailed description of how I would use the money from cost to rent a building, purchase supplies and equipment, and working capital to do things like pay bills and employees. I had some homework to do, and I got started immediately. It took me a bit longer than I would have liked to complete everything, but I was eager to get the application back to the bank and see how much money I would be approved for. The meeting took place February 7, 2020, and one week before I was scheduled to purchase a local moonwalk and party rental business.

TIME TO PLAY CAFE

One aspect of my play café idea that I plan to implement is the option of hosting parties and events both on site and at the customers location. I want to offer unique party entertainment, such as at home board games or trivia night parties, where we provide a variety of games and act as the game master or game host, allowing the party host and guest to sit back, relax, and participate. One thing about game nights and playing certain games is that sometimes one person must be the judge and doesn't get a chance to play. Sometimes they also must decide if a person was right or wrong and earned a point, or if players are playing the game correctly. By acting as game master and judge, we can allow all guests to play carefree and take on the stress of fully understanding the game, teaching the guests how to play, and being the bad guy if or when players disagree.

I began searching the internet looking for existing businesses that owners wanted to sell. There are a variety of websites such as: WeSellRestaurants, BizBuySell,

Transworld Business Advisors, and Franchise Direct that list franchise businesses that you can buy into, like Subway or MyGym, as well as some that you can take over from an existing owner. They also list non franchise individual owned businesses. I scoured these websites looking for cafes and coffee shops for sale and couldn't find anything in my area I was interested in, but out of curiosity I also searched for fun and entertainment-based businesses. I found a K-Pop Karaoke bar in another suburb that seemed promising until the owner flaked. I found an indoor kids' gym that was listed as a franchise-based business but turned out not to be. It was further out than I wanted to travel for work and had a sale price I wasn't willing to pay. I considered a drop-in daycare franchise that sounded like a fun concept and had a supportive management team, but the more I learned about how franchises work the more I realized that wasn't the direction I wanted to go in. On the upside, with a franchise, the company teaches you the ins and outs of running their business model and provides instant name recognition for your company. They also provide training on operating any equipment and do most of your marketing for you. On the downside, they have the final say on what you can and cannot do in the business and what products or services you can and cannot offer. They have final creative control over all marketing, and you must pay them a variety of fees to be a part of the franchise. There is the upfront cost, the ongoing franchise fee, the marketing fees, and I'm sure there are some fees I'm forgetting. None of these things are optional by the way. I didn't want someone else having that much control over how I ran my business; I didn't want to have to ask permission to do things or have anyone restricting my creativity. Another major negative is that there is little room to differentiate yourself from others in your area, and they don't always protect your territory from new franchisee's. Have you ever found it strange that there are multiple Subway sandwich shops within a 5-minute drive of each other? Why should they choose your shop over the one 5 minutes away, when you offer the exact same thing, well most of the time? After my meeting with the bank, I learned that Subway only prevents a new store from opening up in your area for a limited amount of time, which is why multiple Subways exist within a short distance from each other.

OLD SCHOOL

One day I was back at work scouring the websites, when I came across a moonwalk inflatable business that was for sale. I sent an info request form to the broker and after a few days I hadn't heard a word. This was my first time using the system, but I knew eager brokers usually are calling you or sending a non-disclosure agreement (NDA) within hours or a day at most. Some will even call you immediately to explain the business and gage your interest, but not this time. I thought, *Well it's the internet, maybe it got lost in the internet space or that the broker just hadn't seen my request*, so I tried again, and I waited. Again crickets. So, I kept looking and contacting other brokers about other available businesses, like an indoor playground and kiddie gym. I was intrigued by a few of them but was discouraged either by the price or the location. Houston is big, and while a business may be listed in Houston; it could be in one of the many suburbs. I live in one of those suburbs in North Houston, but the businesses I liked were all in places like Sugarland and Katy, which are over an hour away from me. After talking with brokers for the indoor playground, a K-POP karaoke bar, and a cookie store; I

169

determined none of them would be a good fit. Either the price was too high, the space was too small, or the location was outside of my desired area. For my first business, I ideally wanted something close to home, so I passed. Months went by and I saw the moonwalk business was still listed for sale. I decided to do things the hard way and gave the broker listed on the website a phone call to find out why I had never heard back from my multiple inquiries.

When we spoke, he told me that he was old school and his clients expected a certain level of diligence from him, which meant he didn't respond to electronic inquiries; he required in-person meetings before he would even discuss the details of the business with a potential buyer to confirm they were the kind of people his clients would want to do business with. It didn't make a ton of sense because he is a broker selling businesses not trying to create partnerships. I don't know if that is 100% the truth or if he just wasn't super tech savvy and wasn't receiving my request, I mean when we met he had me sign a carbon copy paper NDA, then he printed off pages and pages of documents for me to review— including several years of tax filings for the current owners— instead of just emailing me digital copies. Either way, his old fashioned, look 'em in the eyes and shake their hand approach ended up being to my benefit because no one else had snatched up the business all those months later. Ironically, when I started communicating with the broker by email following that initial face-to-face meeting, the broker accidentally sent emails to me between him and his clients. In the emails, he explained my interest in the business by saying, "At long last I have found a buyer prospect for your business." I'm guessing he could have had more prospects if he had only responded to those electronic inquiries. The email went on to say my offer, which was lower than their initial asking price, was the "first real offer" they had received and that they should consider it very carefully. They had been trying to sell for a long time and despite his efforts to list the business online and in industry specific outlets, they hadn't had much luck. I did some research and consulted with friends and family and decided that I would purchase the company and take it to the next level. I purchased *Bluesky Moonwalks* on February 13th, 2020, my sister Fallon's birthday. Muhammad, who is always down for business ventures, was by my side and agreed to help me make the business a success. During the closing meeting, the former owners showed us how to transfer the MagicJack phone number from their phones to ours. At the same moment the phone rang and we booked our first inflatable rental for the following weekend. The day we picked up all our inventory, Muhammad decided it was a great idea to book a table and chair rental in the middle of loading everything into the largest U-Haul truck available. We were officially in business.

BLUESKY MOONWALKS-MASTER PLAN

Purchasing *Bluesky Moonwalks* was just phase one of my Master Plan. The moonwalk business was supposed to be a revenue stream of my larger business, the play café. I wanted to start making money and be able to have even more cash to put towards collateral for a loan, so that I could bring my full vision to life. One great thing about buying when I did, was that there were jobs already booked that we simply had to execute, and I had someone on the team that was going to make that easier. The previous contract employee, Shady, agreed to stay on and handle most of the delivery and setups. Muhammad and I also went on the first few jobs to get a more hands-on feel and continue learning about the business up close and personal. We rented a box truck from U-Haul and went out to do deliveries. I believe we had three jobs that first weekend. It was a lot to manage, but it was also exciting. We were relying heavily on Shady—who spoke Egyptian Arabic as his first language and English as his second language—to tell us what to do and what we needed. Things were going smoothly, we delivered to our first customer a little early, the setup went great, and they were happy with our service. On top of this their daughter's friends had a great time at her birthday party. The second order should have been the first, based on when the party was supposed to start, but it ended up being farther than the first customer's house, so we arrived maybe 10 or 15 minutes late. I apologized for the delay and the customer immediately asked for some type of compensation. Turns out her party wasn't starting until several hours later, but she still wanted either a discount or extra rental time. I told her I would gladly give her 15% off her total, or she could keep the rental an extra hour. She took the discount. We hadn't taken time to discuss the logistics of making deliveries. Do you deliver to the customer who has an earlier party time or to the customer who is farther away? What if two customers want the same delivery time? We were learning on our feet. The last order was for an evening party, and we arrived with plenty of time to get set up. However, there was an issue with some of the equipment. Inflatables are powered by a plug-in blower that pushes air into a hose which keeps it inflated. Our remaining blower was not working properly, so we had to go back to the warehouse and get a replacement blower.

In the midst of this, Peter, the former owner, called to ask if I was interested in buying the F150 pickup truck they had used for deliveries and suggested we could test it out that day. So, he had the contractor, Shady, meet him at his house and drive the truck to the last job. Since Muhammad is a mechanic, I suggested we take the pickup truck back to the warehouse so he could test drive it. We all jumped in and headed toward the warehouse. A few minutes into the drive, I realized something important. In my haste to get to the warehouse and back to the party as quickly as possible, I had left my keys in the U-Haul truck, and I needed those to open the door to the warehouse. Muhammad had a key as well, so I timidly asked him if he had brought his keys with him. My heart sank and I went into full panic mode when he told me he had left them in the box truck. We started thinking of a plan B. I didn't want to go back to the customers' house and get the key, then drive back to the warehouse. I thought it would #1, make us look unprofessional and #2, take more time. We weren't unprofessional; we were just new to the game, and it was our first day. So, I did a Google search and found out that Home Depot sells the type of blower we needed. We changed directions and headed towards the closest Home Depot in the area. When we got there, we frantically looked for the blower, only to learn they don't carry the blowers in the store; they are only sold online. There was no comparable equipment anywhere in the store; the closest thing we could find was a blower system used to air out wet surfaces. I got another call from Peter, checking to see how everything was going, and what we thought of the truck. I told him about the epic fail with the blower and our efforts to resolve the problem. He explained how they had done the same thing in the past and from then on always brought an extra blower on the jobs just in case. He said Shady should have known that. Okay, on to plan C. We needed a way to get the specialty lock off the door at the warehouse, which isn't technically a warehouse, it's a self-storage unit. They give you these extra secure locks that can't be cut easily with bolt cutters, so Muhammad decided we should buy an electronic power saw thingamajig; no that is not the technical name. On the drive back to the warehouse, Shady and Peter talked on the phone in Arabic, which I don't speak; but I was sure they were laughing at us. The same way you know when the nail tech is talking about another customer as they get out the big tools for their pedicure. We rushed to the warehouse

176

and began feverishly working to cut the lock off and were making no progress. If anything, it seemed we were just damaging the area around the lock but not getting close to cutting through the thick metal. The entire time I'm telling him it's not working, and we should stop wasting time and go back to the customer's home and get the keys. I repeated over and over how it was getting late and the longer we spent trying to get it off and seeing it was not going to work the later, we would be getting back to the party. I began to panic and tear up. I regretted my choice to become a business owner. What the hell was I thinking? I should have tried harder to find another job, I am not a business owner person, I am a worker person! Plan D was to run to the storage center office and see if they had the tools to remove the lock. By the time we thought of plan D, it was already 5 or 6 p.m. and the office was closed. They couldn't help us. No one was coming to save me. And the customer's party was starting in an hour. Okay, Plan E was super embarrassing, but we were out of options. It was time to go back to the customer, explain our screw up, and get the keys. So off we went, me absolutely losing my ish and feeling embarrassed in front of my new employee, but totally unable to do anything about it. We pulled up in front of the customer's house and I was near tears, ready to suggest just giving them a full refund and going home, so I could crawl under my bed. At that moment, Muhammad volunteered to take the heat and go talk to the customer, and I was thankful and anxious to hear how they reacted. Thankfully, they were not even ready to start the party. The mom was in the shower getting ready and didn't even know what was happening. The dad told us it was fine but to hurry back. I finally could breathe a small sigh of relief. We raced back to the warehouse, grabbed another blower, and back to the party as quickly as possible. We did give them a partial refund to make up for the inconvenience. That first day was fun, exciting, and beyond stressful. I was so relieved once I made it home and could get some rest. By the time I went to bed, I wasn't sure if it was all going to work out or if this was a huge mistake.

I wallowed in self-doubt for a few days, but the constantly ringing phone with requests to book bounce houses and waterslides didn't leave me much time for that. I got it together and my excitement rebounded. We were booking jobs using a very manual process. The previous owners had a basic website with a single picture of the items in their inventory, from tables and chairs to moonwalks and waterslides, and the different prices depending on if a customer wanted to rent the item wet or dry. The website was strictly informational and had no interactive ability; customers couldn't click to see more pictures, nor could they check availability of a particular item, find out quantity information, or book an event. Instead, they had to call the phone number listed on the website and tell the owners which item they were interested in and what date they needed it. Then the owners would go to their Yahoo email, look at that date and see if the item was already reserved by someone else or not. Then they would create an event for that date and time on the calendar by typing in the customer's name, address, and order details. It was a cumbersome process and was even more difficult if a customer called and you weren't in front of your computer to access the calendar function. Taking calls manually also meant that if you were busy doing something else and didn't answer the phone, you might lose out on a job to someone else who did pick up the phone or had the ability to book online. Let's be honest, a lot of us would rather not have to talk to a human and prefer to do things digitally over the web or on an app when it is convenient for us. It took a few orders and a few phone calls, but I started getting my stride and getting comfortable with how the business operated. My momentum and business operations came to a screeching halt within a few weeks.

It was the height of spring break and the *Houston Livestock Show and Rodeo* was in full swing. The coronavirus had hit Houston hard. The local county judge, Lina Hidalgo and Mayor Sylvester Turner issued a *Stay Home-Stay Work Safe* order which prohibited all large gatherings. The rodeo was shut down early and special events like *Cirque Du Soleil,* which I had purchased tickets for, were canceled indefinitely. The financial impacts were severe for business owners who relied on the annual multi-day rodeo for a large part of their income. Non-essential businesses were required to stop operating and my little party rental business was put on lockdown.

Initially, we had no idea how serious the coronavirus was going to impact the business. Personally, I thought it might be something like the flu virus and only last a short time, a few weeks, or a month or two max. The news media and government guidance weren't helpful at all. It was unclear which businesses could operate and which businesses were non-essential and had to shut down. The city of Houston had a website we could turn to for information, but it wasn't very detailed, and the chat function wasn't set up for you to talk with a real person. All we could do was select from the pre-created questions and hope it would lead us to a question and answer that fit our situation. I tried to submit a more specific question online to one of those news websites but never received any feedback. We were inundated with emails and text alerts regarding the Covid-19 threat level for Harris County, as well as, any new restrictions or extensions to the *Stay Home-Work Safe* ordinances. The order said things like all *non-essential* businesses must stop operations at their facilities, though employees can work remotely if able to do so. We had no brick-and-mortar facility, so language like this only confused us. We all considered the stay home orders lockdowns. Despite the city saying they weren't as severe as a lockdown and cautioning the public not to use that term. Orders were in effect off and on from the Rodeo cancellation in March through Spring Break until a new order was issued right before the 4th of July. Summer break and especially the 4th of July are two of the busiest times of the year for this type of business. People are home and want to relax and party with friends and family. Sam, one of the other former owners, called to place an order after calling several other moonwalk companies and finding no availability, which I low-key felt some type of way about him calling me as a last resort, but I chalked it up to him wanting something different that his kids hadn't already played on before. Sam lives in a different county and didn't have the same restrictions as Harris County, but I didn't feel comfortable serving him and not serving local customers. The latest stay home restriction from the City of Houston had me questioning if this was mandatory, a strong suggestion from Harris County, or if it even applied to my business. With so much uncertainty, I made the decision not to operate July 4th weekend. I received multiple calls and inquiries from customers wanting to make reservations. The unclear government guidance and my own moral uncertainty made me question if it was appropriate to rent out moonwalks for parties. I wondered if doing so could lead to spread of the coronavirus and how I might be responsible. I decided it was not something I wanted to risk, so I refrained from operating for all of July.

Nobody seemed to know how long a shutdown might last. The moonwalk industry is sort of a niche mar-

ket, because it falls into the entertainment field, which at first glance would make us non-essential. However, many operators including Bluesky, do not have brick and mortar locations, so we didn't have a facility to close. We aren't directly causing crowds and since we typically deliver to homes, we aren't creating a risk of causing a larger gathering. It would be up to the customer how many people they have using the inflatable. On the other hand, we know that if people are renting moonwalks, they are usually doing so for a party, which could make us indirectly responsible for a potential spread. During the pandemic, we received orders from customers that just wanted to entertain their children in their backyard since Spring break was canceled, and most folks had opted not to travel. We took orders on a case-by-case basis, which helped us stay active and learn slowly the first year, but there were many orders we turned down during the on and off stay home orders.

MRS. KNOW IT ALL

After my initial meeting with the previous owners and their responses to all my information seeking questions, I thought there was so much that could be done to see an increase in revenue. I naively thought that I had all the ideas necessary to turn up the heat on the business and start making *mo money, mo money, mo money*. I thought they could be renting out moonwalks multiple times a day instead of doing all-day rentals, because clearly that would quickly and easily boost the revenue. Other moonwalk rental companies offer hourly rates in blocks of 4, 8, 10 hours or more, so it must be possible, right? After communicating with the old owners, I learned that it wasn't actually logistically feasible to drop off a moonwalk or a wet water slide, then pick it up, clean, and sanitize it; then deliver it to another customer on the same day. Once I started receiving orders, I learned that customers typically want to have the moonwalks for as long as possible and as cheap as possible. So, most wouldn't want to just do a few hours rental.

I learned from the old owners that they initially did a variety of advertising. But, at the time of the sale, they were relying exclusively on word of mouth to get business, as well as, sporadically posting on Facebook. They no longer had any paid advertisements. My plan was to start using paid advertisements such as Google and Yelp. I had a call from one of the Google Ads' sales reps to discuss how they could help me start seeing increased traffic to my website, which would hopefully lead to increased sales numbers. She briefly explained how Adwords worked, and how my business could optimize advertisements by selecting specific Adwords. This call took place in the summer during one of the shutdowns. At that point, it didn't make sense to spend money on advertising for a business I wasn't sure I could even operate legally with all the government restrictions. I decided to hold off on starting a Google Ads campaign until we had a better understanding of how the coronavirus was going to impact business in Houston. I did test the waters with some minimal advertising on Facebook but honestly, I didn't know best practices and it didn't appear to have created much traction. Thankfully, the phone was still ringing with interested potential customers.

THE IDEAL CUSTOMER

One thing I've learned in less than two years as a business owner is that not everyone is your ideal customer. Renting a moonwalk for your kid's birthday party will make your child happy, which will make you happy, but you can have a party without one. I am catering to people who are willing to splurge a little on something extra. I want to reach customers that recognize that what they are purchasing is a fun *non-essential,* if you asked the city of Houston, luxury experience.

Shortly after I purchased the company, I made some changes to the pricing. I had a clear rationale for why I made those changes, and I didn't think most folks would notice or that the price increases were substantial or unreasonable. The previous owners had maintained the same prices for the four years they were in business, and they had kept operating costs low in a few ways. They didn't pay for accounting software, they didn't pay for booking software that could be integrated into their website, and they didn't pay for a storage facility. Instead, they booked events manually, and spread out storage of the equipment at the different owners' homes. This isn't the most convenient way to manage your inventory, but it does help the bottom line. The old owners also allowed customers to book events upfront without charging them until the day of the party, which is convenient for the customer but not great for the business cash flow. I inherited this policy and for a while it worked, until it didn't. When a customer books a party and pays nothing down, they have little incentive not to cancel, which costs me money. That may sound strange at first, but if you book an item, say an extremely popular waterslide which rents for $280; and someone else calls to book it for the same date, they can't get it because you reserved it first. I get the same amount of money whether it's from Jack or Jill. Now let's say it's the day before or even worse the day of your pre-scheduled event and you decide you can't do the party for whatever reason. I just lost $280 because it's unlikely I'll be able to rent it to someone else at the last minute. Trust me this has happened several times. Someone calls to reserve an item and I turn them away because it has been booked by someone else. Some customers that previously booked with me and paid cash the day of the event were shocked when I started requiring a deposit to reserve their items. But I had instances where one of those customers made a reservation for the following weekend and then a few days before his party called to cancel because someone else in his family told him they had taken care of booking a bouncer. Well, wouldn't you know the day of his party, he was calling me trying to get a waterslide at the last minute, because the person who said they handled it didn't and now they had no entertainment for their event. I've also had customers tell me that some other company quoted them a lower rate than me, and I still didn't change my price. The price is the price. You are getting quality inflatables and party equipment from *Bluesky Moonwalks*, you are getting great customer service and convenience because we do all the setup and breakdown for your event, and you are getting clean well-maintained equipment.

Luxury costs money and if you don't want to pay the price I charge, it's cool, but the price is the price. I'm charging what I think it's worth and what I need to see a profit. I don't think customers realize what goes into the services we provide. I have to pay for storage space, truck insurance and gas, truck maintenance and repairs, accounting software and credit card processing, booking software, plus phone service so I can receive all those customer calls, and website hosting fees; and all of that is before I even pay my contractors to do delivery and setup of the moonwalks. I also pay for cleaning supplies and for my team to clean the equipment. There is also liability insurance and state inspection fees. All of this before I get a penny. The first year, I didn't pay myself a single penny; no salary, no dividends, the most I've done is treat myself and my delivery team to the occasional company paid lunch. All these costs go into determining how much we charge.

I want customers who see value in luxury, and I want customers who value technology. Some of the customers that were contacting us weren't going to the website. They would want to know what types of rentals we offered, the size of the moonwalks, and the prices. Even though this information was readily available online, they didn't take the time to use the website, some even said they didn't know we had a website. They just looked up moonwalk rentals on Google and started calling different companies. Half of them didn't want to pay what we charged or wanted moonwalks we didn't have. I've had countless calls asking for character bouncers like Princess Tiana, Baby Shark, and other licensed bouncers we didn't have, or wondering if we had any other water slides besides the ones listed on our website. Cause we all know that companies have a secret stash of inventory they only give to customers smart enough to call and ask. It did give me insight into what type of inflatables I should add to my inventory based on the request I received from customers. I'm sure some of this was because the original website was not very functional. *Bluesky Moonwalks* needed a new website that would take some of the manual work off my plate and give more control to the customers.

After learning about different options, I decided to go with a software company called *Inflatable Office,* which automates the booking process for inflatable rental companies. Not only were they going to make it easier for me to manage my inventory, but they would also build a new website that had the interactive do-it-yourself capabilities I wanted to offer my customers. They can get price quotes and even book a reservation without having to call me first. On the backend, it provides me with analytical data on which items rent the most, how much we are making each month, and how well our sales and discount codes are working. The new website and embedded software are a game changer because it also allows me to blackout dates that we aren't going to be operating, as well as create different prices for peak days like 4th of July and Labor Day. Automating much of the process of operating the business and streamlining the work makes it easier for this mostly one woman show to succeed. I still get calls from people with the same questions, I had to accept that this is just the nature of the business. I also still get lots of last-minute calls from customers like my best friend Amanda. She is a spur of the moment, last-minute shopper. She isn't one to book a month in advance or even a week. She isn't going to go to your website. She is going to call you and ask question after question or request you send her a picture, even if you put all the information online. So, when I call her to vent about my frustration with certain customers, she sympathizes with them because they are just like her. They are not my ideal customers, they don't want to book it themselves online, they want to get information while driving in their car and don't have time to look on the website. Then there are those who say, "Well, I can get it for less," which can be extremely frustrating. Frustrating, because I spent a great deal of time, effort, and money building the new website and integrating the booking software to make my life and customers' lives easier by adding functionality and user-friendly interfaces and not everyone is using it. When I get comments like this it tells me two things: those callers are not my ideal customer, and I need to do more to target my ideal customers-tech savvy, proactive consumers, using advertisements. .

WINTER STORM URI

For the most part we enjoy hot sunny days, 80 to 90 percent of the time, and then the rest of the time is rainy, stormy, and on rare occasions cold. The Texas cold isn't anything like the Kentucky cold, but in 2021 it decided to give us a run for our money. I honestly don't watch the news for the weather. I rely on the app on my phone and asking Alexa what's the forecast for today. In mid-February, we started hearing advisories that it was going to be extremely cold and that we needed to cover our plants, bring our pets indoors, and drip our faucets overnight. We don't have any pets, and I had just had a new garden planted, so I decided to say *bismillah* (In the name of Allah) and hope they make it through. I'm from the South, so I have experience dripping faucets. I remember forgetting to drip my faucets one year. I woke up early in the morning to use the restroom, and the water in the bathroom sink wouldn't come out. I went to the kitchen and tried to turn the water on there and the same result. I called the water company and asked them if there was an issue in the area, like maybe a burst pipe or water main break? They told me that there were no known issues in the area and that my pipes must have frozen. They suggested I do whatever I could to warm up the house and to wrap the pipes to help thaw them out. I had to deal with no water to wash my hands or being able to take a shower. Thankfully, I had no damage and within a few hours of running the dryer and heating up the house, I was back in business with running water. My next door neighbors weren't quite as lucky. When I came outside the next morning to go to the bakery, I noticed the shared sidewalk was covered in a sheet of ice and water was rushing out from a pipe on the side of the house. The owners of the bakery owned that house and rented it out to college students. I was able to tell them about the pipe, so that they could call a repairman.

I wasn't trying to deal with that mini crisis again, so when the weatherman said drip your faucets, I diligently obliged by dripping the sink in the kitchen and guest bathroom, my brother's bathroom sink and tub, as well as my master bathroom sink and tub. When we woke the next morning, everything was just as we had left it, we had survived the first night.

I proceeded to go on about my day as usual, working on my laptop in the family room with the TV playing the news in the background. They mentioned some people had lost power to their homes overnight, and I was thankful that we had once again been spared. Posts from my neighbors on the Nextdoor app were pinging one after the other with folks saying they had lost power, and some had also lost water and asking if anyone else had. The news reporters explained that we would be experiencing rolling blackouts that would last anywhere from thirty minutes to a couple hours to help with the surge in need for power. We have been through several storms and in all the different storms, we never lost power, not even when Hurricane Harvey hit Houston in 2017. My dad's brother, Uncle Neal, who lives nearby, called to check on me and told me that they had lost power the night before. My dad called to check on me as well, and I started telling him how we were all good and had no issue. Just as I was counting my blessings, everything shut off. I quickly told him I had just lost power and needed to get off the phone to save my battery just in case. I looked at my phone and it said 4:30 p.m. I figured that it would be a few minutes and then everything would turn back on, that's the typical outage time for us in my neighborhood when we have random power outages. My brother jumped into flight mode and suggested we go to a family friend's house. I wasn't as concerned and told him we should give it a few hours before we leave the house. With no power, he was napping at 5 p.m. I took advantage of the lack of distractions to do some extra writing. I had downloaded a couple of movies on my Kindle the night before and was prepared to keep myself entertained come nightfall. Muhammad wasn't home, so I didn't want to run off and leave him to come home to an empty, dark house, so I waited for him to get back. He called around 6 or 7 to see if we had power and I told him no, but it will probably be back on soon. By about 8 p.m., he was home, and we still had no power. My brother woke up and started discussing going to the family friend's house for the night. We decided we would give it until the next morning and if we still had no power, then we would find somewhere else to go. We methodically went around placing towels in front of every door, trying to keep the cold air out and the warm air in. I filled the big garden tub in my bathroom with water, apparently if the pipes freeze you can pour water into the toilet to force it to flush. I am a planner and preparer, so I took all the suggestions seriously.

Thankfully, Muhammad had just bought this power bank that could charge multiple devices at a time, including cell phones and laptops. We watched a crazy good movie on the Kindle called, *The Lie* and then everyone went to sleep comfortably with extra blankets on the beds and dressed in layers and socks. I never sleep in socks, but that night I managed to keep them on.

The next morning, we woke up to a house a little cooler than when we went to bed and still no lights. Our phones were on the fritz, with text messages coming in sporadically, receiving calls in but not being able to make calls out. The cooler temperature wasn't unbearable, but with no power, we also had no internet and that meant we couldn't get any work done. We decided to get dressed and seek refuge in the warmth of the car. We were hoping to find a coffee shop, restaurant, or somewhere with heat and power while we waited for the electricity to be restored to our neighborhood. Nothing was open since even the businesses had lost power. We tried to call multiple hardware stores like *Harbor Freight, Northern Tools,* and even *Home Depot* to see if they had any generators or kerosene heaters. Nobody answered the phone, so we drove to see if any of them were open. The parking lots were empty except at *Home Depot*. The parking lot was full, and people were standing in a long line out of the front door. Muhammad and I jumped out of the car and prepared to wait in line with the rest of the people. We didn't have to wait long. A store worker came outside and yelled, "We don't have any water, we don't have any generators, and we don't have any kerosene heaters." We turned around and got back in the car. As an adult, I never thought I would be in desperate need of a kerosene heater, not even Amazon could help us.

We drove around until we found a gas station to park in that was getting a strong phone signal. I was able to check my email, browse through Facebook, and get some great writing done, sitting in the passenger seat listening to Lauren Hill and Adele on the radio.

We drove around looking for hotels, just in case we got desperate; but like Mary and Joseph, we found there was no room at the inn. The hotels we came across had white paper signs on the door saying they either were full, sold out, or also had no power. When we got home, the power was still out, but I wasn't really feeling like staying with someone else. My brother was back on his let's go to a family friend's house campaign, but Muhammad said we could "thug it out" another night. My Uncle Neal called to tell me that he still didn't have power by day two. We promised to check in on each other, and if one of us got power we would invite the other and their family over to stay. Donald abandoned ship and went to stay with his friends. Muhammad decided we should cook all the meat in the freezer and warm up our leftover lunch of pizza and wings on the grill along with a pack of hotdogs. It reminded me of cooking food in the fireplace and gathering kindling. We were exhausted and went to sleep too tired to even watch a movie. Just as we were getting comfortable, the lights popped on overhead. I jumped out of my bed, excited to hear the heater kicking on. I looked at my phone and it was 9:30 p.m. We had gone 17 hours without power. I ran into the bathroom, started the shower water, and got all freshened up. I was thrilled to stand under the warmth of the hot water and didn't even care that the house wasn't all the way warmed up yet. I called my brother to let him know the power was back on, and he laughed and told me there was no power at his friend's house, but they were keeping the house warm using heat from the oven. The news had strongly warned against people doing this as it is extremely dangerous and can lead to death. My house is two stories, and the ground floor is an open floor plan, so it would be hard to use this hack to keep the house warm. We would have to sleep in the living room for it to even be slightly helpful. The idea seemed dangerous to me, and I much prefer sleeping in my bed to sleeping on the couch anyway. We still went to bed early but felt so much relief since the power was back. I conservatively set the thermostat to 73 and flipped on my fan to enjoy a peaceful night's sleep.

The next morning, I woke up ready to start the day until Muhammad came in and said, "I think the power is back out." I looked up and saw the fan I had turned on before bed wasn't moving; I realized he was right. I got up and packed a go bag of clothes to last a few days for myself and him. My mother-in-law had invited us to seek shelter in Georgia, and Muhammad's cousin had invited us to her place down in Florida. At this point, we were seriously considering it. Hotels in the city were still full and taking no new bookings, others had no power and had issues with their water, from lack of pressure to no water at all. I put everything I thought we might need in the bag and put it in the corner of the room, so I could get to it easily in the dark. My childhood had prepared me for navigating in these conditions. But in this instance, unlike in my childhood, I could escape the unwelcomed circumstances. I had money to get a hotel, we had gas in the car, hell we could catch a flight if we wanted to. It was inconvenient yes, but not as frustrating as the years and years of unexpected times we had our power turned off for nonpayment. With Muhammad, it was more of an adventure that we were dealing with together, which was comforting. Although as a family, we always experienced the lights off together,we didn't typically talk about it. Even as we got older and realized Momma wasn't handling the finances the way she should, we all dealt with it on our own. Muhammad never dealt with the power being off as a kid, so he doesn't have the insights I do. I told him we should put the suitcase in the car and go back out for the day. I figured it was better to have it with us on the off chance we found a hotel with an opening. We did not find a single hotel. We stayed out all day, working from the car. Heck, I even met with a closing agent at his home to sign refinance paperwork on my home loan. He thankfully still had power. By the time darkness was setting in, we decided we would go home and see if the power had been restored. I checked my security alarm app and saw it was connecting to the internet, which meant we had power at the house. We came home and cooked dinner, assuming that by the next morning we would be in darkness again. When we woke up the heat and lights were still on, but we were anxiously waiting for them to go back out, as part of the supposed rolling blackouts mandated by ERCOT (The Electric Reliability Council of Texas); they never did. The city was able to figure out how to keep the power on in our area.

Texas power lines and pipes are not made to sustain such extreme weather conditions. According to an article by Sami Sparber on March 15, 2021, at least 57 people died and of those 25 were in Harris County, which includes Houston; between February 11th and March 5th. "The majority of verified deaths were associated with hypothermia, but health officials said some were also caused by motor vehicle wrecks, carbon monoxide poisoning, medical equipment failure, falls, and fire." (Texas Tribune 2021)

At the height of the crisis, nearly 4.5 million Texas homes and businesses were without power. That's because nearly half of the total power generation capacity for the main state electricity grid was offline as weather conditions caused failures in every type of power source: natural gas, coal, wind, and nuclear. Millions of Texans went days without power.

Men, women, and children died during this crisis because the people of Texas aren't used to preparing for this type of weather. We are used to battening down the hatches for hurricanes, not snow, ice, and freezing temperatures. Many of us, myself included, were excited when the weatherman predicted snow. I was hoping we would get enough to build a snowman, not the typical flurries we occasionally got over the last 7 years. I thought of how I prepared for snow back home in Kentucky. I went grocery shopping for extra food, in case we were snowed in and couldn't get to the store, canned goods in case we lost power, and snacks because you always need extra snacks, and waited excitedly. For some kids it would be their first-time seeing snow, including Christian an 11-year-old boy who played in the snow for the first time on a Sunday. His family lost power and tried to stay warm by all sleeping in the same room, dressing in layers, and using extra blankets at night. But by Tuesday, when they tried to wake him and couldn't, they realized he was dead. Initially his death was believed to be the result of hypothermia, but an autopsy determined he had died from carbon monoxide poisoning. My initial excitement for snow didn't account for the potential devastation that the storm could cause.

Living in Houston, we don't typically deal with the same seasonality concerns other areas face because it's mostly sunny and hot year-round, aside from the rainy season. Even in the Fall/Winter months, we have high temps in the 60s and 70s, so moonwalk rentals can still be active, but the orders aren't as high as the summer and spring months. I decided that with slower sales, it was not the time to begin paid advertising. January and February of 2021 were extremely slow, and the winter weather was severe, setting record lows with temps in the single digits. The state of Texas and especially Houston, came to a screeching halt due to frozen roads, lack of electricity, heat, and running water. Sales were non-existent but things turned around in the 3rd week of February, thanks to improved weather conditions and increased cash in the economy because of stimulus checks and income tax returns.

In the Spring, I began investing in new equipment and started promoting the business more on Facebook and Google. All the requests I received last year that we couldn't fulfill had been floating around in my mind. I did lots of internet window shopping and compared prices to find the best manufacturer to supply me with new moonwalks and waterslides. Since I have new equipment, I think this is a great time for moving forward with paid advertising. I'll have something exciting to share with customers both new and existing, as the revitalized *Bluesky Moonwalks*.

While the business floated the first year, I didn't set any records or make the kind of money we anticipated based on the previous years. But 2020 was a year like no other year and I am remaining optimistic. The impact of the coronavirus may last another year, but as a nation, we have started to move forward with a new normal, and people are still having events and looking for forms of entertainment. I think we can be a part of that. I'm pushing myself to stop holding back due to uncertainty and fear, but instead make carefully thought out and strategic moves in multiple aspects of my business. The adage, *You have to spend money to make money,* is true. I had to spend money to purchase my moonwalk business and I have spent money on storage of my equipment, insurance, and wages for my contract workers. As I mentioned, I haven't yet paid myself and thankfully have had other sources of income to sustain me, but in 2021 I want to change that. A lot of what I have done has been winging it, trying to do as much as I can on my own because I didn't feel like I could afford to pay anyone else. Now I am preparing to invest in more support for the business, such as increasing my staff pool of contractors, bringing on an accountant to help me manage the books, and of course paying for advertising, hiring someone to assist me with social media marketing, and managing emails. I get to determine what my brand is and how to let other people help me shape that brand.

NO MAN OR WOMAN IS AN ISLAND

> *One of the saddest things is when someone struggles alone to do something to prove to others, they can do it. You don't have to do that stuff all by yourself! Get some help, get clear, and get to action!—Zarinah El-Amin*

I have wanted my own business for years, and I naturally assumed that my family would be a part of it and would help me achieve my vision. When I was in high school, I had this idea to design modest casual clothing that would appeal to Muslim women. There are a bunch of cute, casual, faith-inspired clothing. Some of the options I have seen is t-shirts with words like faith, believe, a cross, or something along those lines; but when I mentioned wanting to do something similar for Muslim women, I couldn't find the resources I needed to make it happen. I was sixteen or seventeen and didn't know anyone who made shirts or anyone in the clothing industry. Years later, these items are prevalent in mainstream shopping channels. Mark and I were talking recently, and he told me how he wishes the family had listened to me and helped me bring my clothing idea to life. It made me feel good to hear that and I think if I had pushed it more back then, the family would have supported me and helped me figure out what I needed to do.

When I decided to start my business in 2020 and have the self-managed 401K, I learned that I had to have a board of directors. My first thought was to put my family on the board in name only, not thinking they would want to be involved. They have their own jobs and lives, and this was my idea. I, of course, told them and gave everyone titles. My brother Mark is Vice President. My sister Fallon has a degree in Communication, so I made her Secretary. My nephew Jared holds several degrees, including one in Business Communication and a Bachelors in Nursing. He also has previous experience in finance. He is the Treasurer. I haven't had a formal meeting with my board and haven't asked them for advice on any of my business decisions. I finally asked Fallon to help me manage the monstrosity of my emails. Part of me hasn't wanted to bother anyone, and the other part of me hasn't known how to ask for help. I've been winging it day-to-day and hoping for the best. In 2021, I plan to put my board members to work and consider adding people that are not family. I think they will be willing to help me be successful and happy to be a part of that success. I just need to be open to suggestions, criticism, and recognize that true success isn't likely to come from me all alone.

> *No man is an island, entire of itself;*
> *every man is a piece of the continent, a*
> *part of the main.—John Donne*

And I have realized that I don't have to make it happen all on my own. I am open to coaching and mentoring from anyone with experience in business. Just as I believe in getting a coach to help me write my first and hopefully future books. I have also joined industry groups to get inside information on the moonwalk and party rental industry because I realize the value in other people's knowledge, opinions, and experience.

Losing my job was not how I anticipated starting a business. Ideally, I would have liked to keep working a full-time job and have that stability, security, and benefits that working for an established company provides. I would have had my passion project or projects on the side and then once the income from a passion project reached a level high enough to sustain my financial responsibilities, then I would have been able to consider leaving my job. But being pushed to establish something of my own has also made me eager to explore all the possibilities for ways to make money that I ever had an interest in. I don't necessarily recommend that, but it has been my method. Not having a *regular* job has given me the freedom and time to explore different possibilities, including writing this book. Writing this book has sparked thoughts about jobs that would allow me to use more of my creative side, like being a voice artist.

If someone were to ask me, a non-expert, what my suggestions would be on how to start a business, I would caution them to not just quit a stable job while venturing into business ownership. It takes a long time to start making a profit, and the world and business ownership can be unstable. I would encourage them to save, save, and save some more, for the times when the orders are not coming in or when the bills outweigh the incoming dollars. Do plenty of research on the business you are interested in and start surrounding yourself with experts in the field. Learn the different ways to fund a new business, from self-funding through saving your own money, seeking a partner or partners to financially back the venture, to crowdfunding, as well as seeking either a business or personal loan. If you do choose or are forced to start a business after losing a job that offers a 401k, talk to your tax professional or a CPA about how you can legally use these funds penalty free to finance your own business. It's good to know all your options as soon as possible to determine which direction is best for you and your funding needs. If you are going to start a business that requires supplies or equipment, such as a party rental business, think about how you can purchase those items. Do you want to be debt free and buy everything with cash or can you save money by financing these purchases and maintaining cash liquidity? Initially, I was very opposed to financing equipment purchases because I was fortunate enough to have enough cash reserves in the bank due to financing my business using funds from my 401k from my prior job. I didn't want to have any debt or deal unnecessarily with interest from purchasing equipment on credit. Now I realize that there are benefits in financing these purchases and can also help establish business credit, which can in turn help you to obtain even more financing, such as an SBA loan.

BLACK MAGNOLIA COLLECTIVE

One night in the middle of 2020, I had a dream where I was holding a pretty piece of paper like a stationary, and on that paper I saw the words Black Magnolia. When I dream about something interesting, I wake up and make a note of it on my phone. Immediately, I knew that Black Magnolia was something special. In the morning, I Googled black magnolia and was flooded with images of deep purple flowers, a type of tulip. The flowers are absolutely beautiful. They give me southern elegance and royalty vibes. So, I filed away the beauty and the name for future use.

Since the first year has been slower than expected with the moonwalk business, and I can't yet open my play café, I decided to revisit my earlier dream of having a clothing store. My Facebook friend, Faheemah, has owned her own online boutique Glitter & Goon LLC. for a few years now, and I admire her drive and the success she has had with her business. Faheemah is not just a Facebook friend, she is also a creative business associate that I have worked with multiple times to help design my logos for *Time to Play Café* and for *Bluesky Moonwalks*. She easily translates my thoughts and examples into an image I love every time. Recently, she started offering a service called *T-Shirt Biz in a Box,* to teach others how to create their own online t-shirt business using the drop shipping method. I was hesitant at first, so I did some homework. I read up on what she offered, watched the videos she made explaining what the *T-Shirt Biz in a Box* service was, and had a video consultation with her. Our conversation was great, her energy and excitement, and transparency about the potential of the business made me move forward with this dream. I began keeping notes on my phone of different t-shirt design ideas, capturing screenshots of t-shirts I liked and anything I thought might make a nice design. One of the homework items she gave me was to start thinking about my brand and what I would call it.

The Black Magnolia name I had dreamed of months earlier seemed like a perfect fit for a boutique. But the depth and vibrancy of that name seemed too small to contain to a single business, so I decided to instead make it the umbrella name for several ventures that are interrelated, so I added the word collective. I created an LLC which could separate this business from my moonwalks and limit my liability. Black Magnolia Collective LLC will house not only an online clothing boutique, but also an event rental venue.

I've been working steadily with Faheemah and will be launching my online boutique in the Summer of 2021 with just shy of 30 t-shirt designs, as well as some great accessories. More than a decade after my initial thought of having a clothing company, it is finally coming to life. My passion and excitement for the boutique is high. I am putting a great deal of thought and effort into the designs and marketing ideas. I finally figured out what my giveaway item will be to get customers to join the mailing list, and that feels amazing. I am not rushing to market with anything I don't love. I've even scrapped a t-shirt idea, after thinking on it. I decided it didn't feel authentic to me. I'm doing my best to establish a clear brand in my head and translate that into every aspect of my business: designs, website, and social media. There is still a degree of fear that says, *What if you put in all this time, effort, and money and it doesn't work? What if nobody buys a single item?* But mostly, I'm excited to see if other people love what I come up with and connect with it enough to want to buy. I try to ignore those whispered thoughts of doubt and replace them with prayers. I pray for inspiration and success often, not just for the boutique but for all my endeavors.

DREAM DEFERRED

I spent over 6 months researching information for starting a play café. I had conference calls with coffee vendors and others I met in person. I contacted playground equipment manufacturers and distributors to find the perfect equipment to meet my vision of inclusive play for children of all abilities. I was constantly online searching for different options and suppliers and receiving quotes. It was an overwhelming time, but it was also an exciting experience. I wrote up a business plan that I revised, and revised, and revised again; changing pricing and adjusting the business operating start date. I kept thinking the shutdown we were experiencing in Houston would be short lived. I was optimistic that I would get approved for SBA funding and then could open my play café. Once I was able to reconnect with the local SBA loan manager, my optimism was dulled. She explained that the economic impact of the stay home orders had been severe for restaurants and food-based businesses. They aren't currently able to offer any new loans to anyone with a food-based concept. I can't get a loan from UNITY National Bank.

I had considered purchasing a *Hard Bean Coffee* franchise and using that as the basis of my play café business. The beauty of this business is that it's not the typical franchise model where you pay ongoing royalties and fees. Instead, you pay a set price for a business in a box. They provide you with all the supplies and equipment, furniture and fixtures, and help build out your location, and then come and train you on how to operate the café. They also allow you full creative control on pricing and naming your business and products. So, you have the option to use the *Hard Bean Coffee* name, or you can name your business something entirely different and indicate that your coffee is *powered by Hard Bean*. That freedom was what appealed to me the most. Once I learned that I couldn't get the funding from my local bank, I contacted the Sales Director, Joel and sought his advice on the next steps. He gave me contact info for some banks they had referred other clients to, to obtain funding. The purchase price of the *Hard Bean* franchise is a flat $149,500. That price doesn't include any operating cost, that doesn't cover paying employees, rent and utilities, or any other monthly expenses. That $149,500 solely covers buying the business in the box. My vision is broader than just a coffee shop. I also want to offer play and entertainment. I need funds to cover board games, a play structure, karaoke equipment, and such. So, with all things considered, I anticipated needing a loan for a minimum of $300,000 to even get started with my full vision. I reached out to the brokers and explained my business concept and the amount of money I wanted to borrow. Then I completed a preliminary application and provided a copy of my credit report.

I waited on edge for a loan approval amount, checking my email repeatedly. I was shocked when the first broker told me they weren't comfortable with the loan amount I was requesting based on my debt to income, and lack of secondary income. It didn't matter that I had over 30 grand to use as a cash injection and 7 grand in personal savings. So not only do they want you to have a full-time job and substantial funds for a down payment, they also want you to make sure the business is successful.

The Sales Director for *Hard Bean* had given me a lengthy list of banks to apply with and so I started contacting other banks on the list and found Lisa. She suggested I apply for an unsecured commercial loan. The unsecured loan was solely based on my credit score and credit profile and didn't require any cash down payment, collateral, bank statements, or years in service for the business. It made getting approved a more efficient process. According to her, the impact of the virus on businesses had made banks much more cautious in their lending. After maybe a day of anxiously waiting for approval, I received an email from Lisa. I was approved for a whopping $25K. I was shocked at the small amount, especially considering my excellent credit score. Apparently, my 700+ score wasn't enough, my credit profile—which I didn't really understand—was the problem. She asked if I had a credit partner. I don't have a list of wealthy family members or friends, and I don't know many people who have a higher credit score than me. Even if I did, I didn't want to risk someone else's name, credit, or money on my dreams. I spoke with Lisa on the phone, and she said basically, I was a victim of bad timing. Applying in the current environment, I would be approved for half of what I would have been had I applied prior to the pandemic. So that $300,000 I was seeking for an SBA loan, I would be lucky to get $150,000, and that's of course contingent on me finding a bank that would consider a food-based business and wouldn't be concerned about my lack of previous experience. At this point, I felt defeated and out of options. I realized my dream of opening a play café would have to be deferred until the pandemic subsides and banks begin loaning to businesses like mine. It was and is a difficult reality to face after investing so much time and energy into this idea and running into wall after wall. I found it difficult to stop looking for the perfect space, and still from time to time will save potential locations to my favorites on Loopnet. I contemplate how I would run my café if it were open. I plan events in my head and feel both excitement and pain when I browse my play café Facebook groups with ladies who are open and having both successes and difficulties. I long to be sharing my journey, my ups and downs, and giving and receiving suggestions. It is at the forefront of my mind, but I am also mindful of the benefits of the position I am in right now.

There are ladies in my play café Facebook groups who are struggling to make ends meet. Some cannot pay their rent or have had to fight with landlords for a rent reduction due to capacity restrictions that limit how many customers they can have. Less customers equals less income to pay the rent. There are those who pivoted successfully to selling activity kits customers can enjoy at home, others were not so successful with this idea. A few just focused on selling curbside coffee at the height of the stay home orders, when they couldn't have customers on site. There are ladies who have had to permanently shut down their business due to the economic impact of the pandemic. One lady was an inspiration for so many of us, but despite her best efforts she had to close her doors as well. There are those who have been fighting to get government assistance such as the Paycheck Protection Program (PPP) loans, the Economic Injury Disaster Loan

(EIDL) program, and various grants; just to pay their bills and employees. There are some like me who never opened because they couldn't get loan approval, so they continue to dream and prepare for that special day. Sometimes I think those of us who haven't started our cafés are the lucky ones.

We are lucky in that we don't have to deal with the stress of not being able to pay the bills or staff. We don't have to fight with landlords about money we don't have or with banks trying to get loans and grants. We don't have to stress about capacity limits, social distancing, or the next shutdown. I try to tell myself how lucky I am in all of this, sometimes it works and sometimes I just can't wait to see my dream come to life. Hopefully, it won't take as long as my t-shirt idea. There has been benefit in having more time to plan and watch the journey of other owners and would-be owners. Although I have had to put my dream on hold for this last year, I am actively searching for the perfect location with high ceilings for my future play structure and green space for outdoor events. Today, March 6th I think I may have found it. We did a drive-thru viewing and just sort of peeped in the windows seeing as much as we could of the main space and the patch of greenery inside of the dilapidated brown wood fence which had as many boards missing as it did still there. I climbed through a large hole next to the locked gate to peek in the window to get a better view of the former daycare. The surrounding area is ideal for my business concept. There is a church and university directly across the street, as well as an elementary school down the road and a large residential community. Even though the space isn't completely ready to go, it is one of the best places I've seen thus far. I was ready to compromise on my must have green space and now I've possibly found a space that meets my wish list. I came home and emailed my realtor requesting she schedule an in-person viewing.

I'm getting ready to start the whole SBA loan process over again and if that doesn't work, I am open to applying for a personal loan. I'm reimagining how to stair step my dream and realize it in parts. I'm pretty much an all at once, all or nothing kind of girl, so it's been hard accepting that it may not go exactly how I originally planned, but that's okay. I may come up with something that's even better at the end of the day. I know this deferment is temporary.

14. Take Away Message

Life is full of things we cannot control. What we can control is how we choose to look at them. When I look back on my childhood experiences, I realized I mostly chose to make the best of things and even our struggles were adventures that we survived together. Sometimes we get consumed by our hard times and think it will always be this way. When we are in the middle of the storm, it is sometimes difficult to see our way out. The best way I have found to deal with these difficult times is to #1, have good company. Sitting in the dark, riding out the wind, rain, and thunder is never as bad when you have someone else beside you. I always had my family. Then there is #2, remember that you get to decide how you respond to anything, you can decide that you want to accept defeat, poverty, and brokenness, or you can decide you will try harder, operate differently, and imagine something greater, and #3, you can take risks.

My hope is that you will start seeing more opportunities, where others see obstacles. I faced many obstacles in my childhood, from moving repeatedly and growing up in a single parent home, to having an almost nonexistent relationship with my father. I was a girl who lived in poverty, grew up seeing drug and gambling addictions, the depths of which I only scratched the surface of in this book. But I rose above it all, graduating from college not once but twice. I went from a girl who lived in the projects to a homeowner, not once but twice. I went from making $5.15 an hour to $55,000 a year, to owning my own businesses. My life is far from perfect and I have had my fair share of struggles, but I have also had my share of successes that most people wouldn't imagine were possible for someone with my background. If I can do it, in spite of everything, then there is hope for anyone facing hardships, including you.

About the author

Katrina Renea is from the beautiful "Bluegrass" state of Kentucky and is the youngest and undeniable favorite of seven children. In her first book *In Spite Of: A Memoir of Family Secrets, Professional Struggles*

and Personal Success, she breaks her mother's rule "what happens in this house stays in this house," sharing childhood memories including some that were never meant to be spoken of outside of the house; hungry days and dark nights, stories of drug and gambling addiction, life hacks, and unexpected blessings. Additionally, she offers insight from her college life, experiences in the corporate world, and present-day struggles and successes as a business owner. She hopes to give readers a glimpse at how she didn't let her past hold her back. She holds both a Bachelor of Science degree and aMaster of Arts in Communication from the University of Louisville and Spalding University, respectively. She spent 12 years moving up the ranks in corporate America at a top health insurance company before pursuing business ownership.

To contact Katrina email her at:
katrinareneawrites@yahoo.com

Bluesky Events Studio

Made in the USA
Middletown, DE
19 September 2021

48640075R00135